Hello Holy Spirit

By Uebert Angel

Published by: LEVI HOUSE

Unless otherwise stated, all scripture quotations are taken from the King James Version of the Bible.

ISBN **978-0-9958499-6-2**

Copyright 2018 by Uebert Angel

Published by LEVI HOUSE

Printed in the United Kingdom of Great Britain. All rights reserved under International Copyright law. Contents and or cover may not be reproduced in whole or in part in any form without the express written consent of the publisher

CHAPTER ONE

The Holy Spirit in My Room!

The visitation happened on a bright sunny afternoon in October, exactly seven days before the British public celebrated Halloween, and three days before our 'Holiness' themed conference. The contrast could not be any sharper!

You see it may be even harder for Halloween fans to believe, but every October after that is more than just spiders, silly strings, pumpkins, and dressing up as zombie brides. For me, October 24 has a special space in my heart. It is the afternoon I came into contact with the Person of the Holy Spirit, and I mean literally. The week of October 24 was the week I least expected to receive a visitation. What happened on that October day changed my world and destiny.

It was a bright sunny afternoon, except for the cold draft of soft wind that twirled the sun's rays until they confused themselves above the British skies. The air was warm, the beams of sunlight glowing on the skin, the sweet aroma of ripening peaches in the orchards was in the air, and the sounds, sights, and smells gently filled the senses making that October afternoon quite tranquil. I could even hear the shuffling scraping sounds of joggers' sneakers on public gravel sidewalks in my farm deep in the neck of the woods of Barnby in the Willows in Nottinghamshire. I could tell, this was a different afternoon.

The Holy Spirit Invades My House

Suddenly, a glow of white filled every inch of where the door should have been. Liquid light with a life of its own invaded my house. The light moved from deep white to brilliant white. It was as if all the universe's atoms in the material world had simultaneously exploded near my door, converting their mass to quanta or light. The sight reminded me of fireworks that have a primary exploding core which sends out comets which themselves explode. The process of these seeming explosions of indescribable light continued until the light was so overwhelming to such an extent that all space in my room became a sea of light. Then as fast as it had started, it transformed into a liquid light Being in the shape of a living being. I remained glued to my seat, not out of fear but in anticipation. I was filled with great and indescribable awe.

The Being sat down in the seat just opposite mine. My skin nearly jumped off my flesh as I was being enveloped in an ocean of supernatural light of the extreme kind. My body was trembling with awe, and before I got a chance to calm down, the supernatural Being spoke in a very serene but powerful voice.

"I am the Holy Spirit."

What? How can the Holy Spirit come like a person? Is He not like wind? Is He not like fire? Is He not like water? All sorts of wonder filled my mind. At the same time, the peace I was experiencing ushered me into a high level of comprehension. Right then and there I was filled with understanding and wisdom. The Holy Spirit began to expound scripture upon scripture, proof upon proof of the secrets of His Power and how christians can partner with Him. During what seemed to be two hours of visitation, the Holy Spirit taught me another dimension of cooperating with Him that forever changed my life and the way I viewed Him. It was a brilliant afternoon, the best in my life I must say. That was the day I learnt how not to fear the Holy Spirit and how not to quench Him and said, "*Hello, Holy Spirit!*"

Understanding the Holy Spirit, My Companion

The Spirit of God told me that afternoon that God has made all power in Heaven and Earth available to those who believe. With this power, the devil and his cohorts are sent bowing. Angels, demons, powers, dominions, all stand at attention when we come in the power of the Spirit. But if we quench the Spirit of God, we will be the ones to stand at attention while the devil calls the shots. It is therefore of great importance for us as the offspring of God Himself to know how not to quench the Spirit. We should learn how to cooperate with the Holy Spirit and flow in His power to perform miracles, signs, and wonders. We should learn how to keep the fire of the Spirit burning rather than pour water on the flames of the Holy Spirit and quench Him.

For this reason, Apostle Paul gives us two related instructions in two different scriptures. In Thessalonians he says:

1 Thessalonians 5:19
Quench not the Spirit.

In Ephesians he also says:

Ephesians 4:30
And grieve not the Holy Spirit...

There is something I don't want you to miss right there. You see, when read in context, these scriptures are saying the same thing but in stages. The Holy Spirit is grieved, and as a result of the grieving, He is then quenched. These scriptures show that the grieving of the Spirit and the quenching of the Spirit work towards one and the same thing. To really understand what I am talking about here, read the verses that follow Ephesians 4:30 up through Ephesians 5:21, and read the verses preceding 1 Thessalonians 5:19 starting from verse 12. You will see that these two passages present the same message.

The Spirit of Love

The Holy Spirit came and set up His headquarters in you the moment you were born again. You are the centre of His operations. He lives in you. Some Christians don't realise that, but the Bible tells us that He has been given to every christian. In fact, there is no Christianity without Him. The Word of God makes that plain when it says:

Romans 8:9
Now if any man have not the Spirit of Christ, he is none of His.

It is the Holy Spirit in you that makes you a bona fide child of God. He is the One who makes the presence and nature of God real to you and in you, and the totality of God's nature is love. For the Bible says:

1 John 4:16
And we have known and believed the love that God hath to us. *God is love* [emphasis added]; and he that dwelleth in love dwelleth in God, and God in him.

God is love! That emphatic statement is communicating far more than just His ability to love. It means that He is love personified, and the Holy Spirit of God is the One who makes the love of God known to us. Apostle Paul puts it this way:

Romans 5:5
Because the love of God is shed abroad in our hearts by the Holy Ghost which is given unto us.

It is through the Holy Spirit that the love of God comes to you. He is the Spirit of love, and everything about Him embodies the love of God. That is essential for us to understand because to walk in the Spirit, we must walk in love.

The Fruit of the Spirit

Everything that comes from the Holy Spirit is a product of love including the fruit of the Spirit. There are not nine fruits of the Spirit as many believe. I know I just messed up someone's theology right there, but it's the truth. Galatians speaks of the "fruit" of the Spirit not the fruits of the Spirit. Let's look at it:

Galatians 5:22-23
But the fruit of the Spirit is love, joy, peace, longsuffering, gentleness, goodness, faith, meekness, temperance: against such there is no law.

The fruit of the Spirit is singular, and that fruit is love. By definition, the word 'fruit' refers to a single kind of fruit, like an orange for example. On the other hand, 'fruits' refers to different kinds or types of fruit. So, when the Bible speaks of the fruit of the Spirit, it is not talking about different kinds of fruit; it is referring to one specific fruit which is love.

That love is manifested in different ways. I call these the components or segments of love. Let me explain using the same example of an orange. When you look at an orange, you will see different segments which make up the orange. We do not look at each of those segments as if they are different kinds of fruits. We call the one fruit comprised of each of those different segments an orange. In the same way, love is the fruit which has different segments or components: joy, peace, longsuffering, gentleness, goodness, faith, meekness, temperance. I hope you're getting this because it is crucial to your relationship with the Holy Spirit.

This fruit of love is what the Holy Spirit produces in you, in your recreated spirit; it is the result of His presence in your life. These qualities will be evident as you walk in fellowship with the Spirit. Walking in the Spirit is walking in love. The converse is also true.

Hello Holy Spirit

When you are not walking in these characteristics of love, you are no longer walking in the Spirit. Instead, you will be grieving and quenching Him. To avoid that, Apostle Paul gives us instructions in 1 Thessalonians 5:12-18 and 20-22 that if followed keep us walking in love and consequently, not quenching the Spirit.

As we examine these verses in 1 Thessalonians 5 more closely in the chapters that follow, you will see that the instructions given in each verse are satisfied by walking in some aspect of the personal qualities which our spirits produce as we fellowship with the Spirit in love. Doing so enables us to maintain our fellowship with the Holy Spirit and not quench Him. However, to know how not to quench the Spirit, we should first understand that there is a big difference between resisting the Spirit and quenching the Spirit. Many in the Body of Christ today have neglected this most important fact, and as a result, the Church is functioning as if it is devoid of the power of God.

As the Holy Spirit sat across the room from me that day, it was as if my mind had just been opened up to understand scripture for the first time. Things that I thought I knew for years began to make sense as He began to show me the manifestation of the Spirit in the Word and in my own life. In fact, even the writing of this book has taken me longer than usual because I had to keep revising each chapter so that I can impart to you the understanding or revelation I received that day.

As I sat there, He would show me in scripture how He is the manifestation of the love of God and what it means when the Bible says that the love of God is shed abroad in our hearts by the Holy Ghost. Then just when I thought I had the whole thing figured out, He went on to say,

"That's why there is no demonstration of power without Me."

The Holy Spirit and Power

That single statement opened up a whole new dimension of revelation. Usually, when we as christians talk about the Holy Spirit, we refer to the power of God. I never understood how His power works until, at that moment, He began to illuminate my understanding through the Scriptures. Watch what the Bible says:

Matthew 14:14
And Jesus went forth, and saw a great multitude, and was moved with compassion toward them, and He healed their sick.

I don't want you to miss this, so I will break it down for you. Before the miracles—before the blind could see, before the lame could walk, before the lepers in the crowd could be healed—something had taken place. The Bible says that when Jesus saw the multitude, He was moved with compassion. Now the Greek word translated as 'compassion' in that passage is *splankna*. The King James version of the Bible actually robs us of the true meaning of that word because its significance surpasses our general understanding of compassion. *Splankna* literally means to have the bowels yearn within you.

That is what it means when the scripture says Jesus was "moved with *compassion* toward them." The Lord Jesus was so sensitive to the Spirit of God to the extent that He could be moved by the love of God in this way, then the power of God would be released, and miracles would happen. It was as if there was an explosion of God's love flowing in Him and causing the healing to come forth. I mean I had never quite made the connection, but the penny had just dropped.

Immediately the Holy Spirit reminded me of one of the Good News conferences we had in Zambia. I remembered it so vividly because we witnessed many miracles that the Lord was working in that place. It was awesome! I remember during that crusade there was a mother who pushed her way through the crowds with a baby in her arms. I will never forget the look on her face. Tears were streaming down her cheeks, and she looked as if the whole world had just caved in on her.

It was at that moment the Lord ministered to me that the baby she was holding had died a few hours earlier, and she had come to the crusade as her last hope. My heart broke as I looked at this sobbing mother. I wished I could take that pain away from her. I didn't know what to do so I looked to the Lord to help this woman. I remember taking that child from his mother's arms, and with thousands in the stadium watching, I laid him on the ground. At that moment, my mind was completely unaware of anything else that was going around me except what the Lord was directing me to do.

I laid across the child covering him three times, and then the Lord told me to give him back to the mother. I picked him up and handed him back to his mother and immediately the lifeless body began to cough, and the whole stadium erupted in celebration.
It was as if the Lord had been watching the memory on the screen of my mind with me, and when it came to an end He said to me,
"The only reason I could work that miracle through you that day is that you were sensitive enough to be moved by compassion, and just like it happened in Matthew 14:14, My power was released."

He continued,
"If you read your Bible, you will find that I even said many times that I am the power of God, and in all the miracles that you read about, I was at work."

Everything that the Lord Jesus would do the Holy Spirit was doing. Another revelation was about to unfold.

Acts 10:38
How God anointed Jesus of Nazareth with the Holy Ghost and with power: who went about doing good, and healing all that were oppressed of the devil; for God was with Him.

Jesus was anointed with the Holy Spirit "and" (*kahee* in the Greek) power. The word *kahee* means 'the mother of.' In other words, we could read that scripture as, "How God anointed Jesus of Nazareth with the Holy Ghost the mother of power: who went about doing good, and healing all that were oppressed of the devil; for God was with Him." Are you getting it now? Watch what the apostle Paul says in his letter to the Roman church:

Romans 8:11
But if the Spirit of Him that raised up Jesus from the dead dwell in you, He that raised up Christ from the dead shall also quicken your mortal bodies by His Spirit that dwelleth in you.

The apostle Paul was teaching us in that passage of scripture that you cannot have the Holy Spirit and not have power. The scripture says, "if the Spirit of Him that raised up Jesus from the dead dwell in you." In other words, if you have the Person of the Holy Ghost living in you, He has an ability to revitalise and rejuvenate your mortal bodies. Anyway, I'm getting way ahead of myself here. There is something else I want us to look at before we get any deeper into this subject.

Quenching vs. Resisting the Spirit

Christians can either cooperate with the Spirit of God or, as powerful as He is, they can quench the Spirit. The world resists the Holy Spirit, but only christians can quench Him. It is of the utmost importance for christians to understand that if we are ignorant of the requirement of the Word of God concerning this issue, that

Hello Holy Spirit

can lead to us quenching the Holy Spirit. By that I mean we can literally put the fire of the Holy Spirit out. Think about all the miraculous things you have been praying for God to do in your life. It may be the only reason you have not yet seen the manifestation of any of it is that you have been putting out the fire of the Spirit. The imagery used by the Apostle Paul is that of pouring water on a burning flame. That imagery is troubling, hence Apostle Paul's explicit directive, "**Do not quench the Holy Spirit!**"

The non-christians in the world resist the Holy Spirit when they reject so great salvation. When they reject the message of the Gospel and refuse to let the Holy Spirit work in their lives, they resist the Holy Spirit. However, because the Holy Spirit is already burning in the life a christians, when we do not accept God's directions upon our lives, we put the fire out completely.

It should also be noted that though Apostle Paul's image of putting the fire out by pouring water on it is of value, it also carries within it an even more profound image of putting cold water on a person in high spirits. This imagery depicts angering a jovial person to the point where that person moves from a state of being joyous or jubilant to a state of retreat; the person becomes reserved and stops speaking. It paints a picture of forcing a person to withdraw from participating.

The Holy Spirit Has Emotions

That imagery of forcing a person to withdraw concurs with the Lord Jesus' emphasis on the Holy Spirit being a 'He' and not an 'it' when He said:

John 16:13
Howbeit when He, the Spirit of truth, is come, He will guide you into all truth.

Some christians still refer to the Holy Spirit as an 'it,' and that's a mess! If the Holy Spirit is an 'it' or simply a power, then we would make that power an errand boy. Some christians even try to send Him to do their will. But if we understand that the Holy Spirit is a 'He,' then we would want to surrender to Him and co-operate with Him. If we think of Him as a force that we refer to as an 'it,' we would want to get a hold of it, but if we understand that He is a 'He,' we would want Him to get a hold of us and be humbled that His love is in us.

Since we now know that the Holy Spirit is a He and not an it, He should of necessity have characteristics ascribed to Him as a Person with a personality and feelings. As such, He is also subject to being grieved or being quenched when He is hurt, ignored, insulted, or offended.

The word 'grieved' is the Greek word *lypéō* meaning to be sorrowful, sad, distressed, made sorry, cause grief, cause heaviness, vex, torment, cause offence, insult, or cause pain to. The Holy Spirit has emotions and can experience deep, intense, severe emotional pain. He can be insulted or grieved. He can be quenched.

When Apostle Paul wrote 1 Thessalonians 5:19, He was giving this information exclusively to the christians and not non-christians because christians are the only ones who can quench the Spirit of God. The non-christians resist Him, but christians can torment, make sorrowful, vex, cause heaviness, offend, insult, and cause deep pain to the Holy Spirit to the extent where His fire can be put out. Grief is the first stage and then the second is quenching. These stages do not happen gradually. As you grieve the Holy Spirit, you immediately trigger a spiritual button to put out the fire of the Holy Spirit. Grieving the Holy Spirit then is the button we press in order to quench the Spirit. There is, therefore, no quenching of the Holy Spirit without grieving Him. There is also no grieving that will not cause quenching of the Spirit.

The word 'quench' is rendered from the word *sbénnymi* which means to snuff out, to make to go out, or to extinguish a fire to the extent where no sign of fire shows. Christians can grieve the Holy Spirit to the point of extinguishing Him from burning in their lives by actions that I, by the Holy Spirit, will expose in this book.

God's View

Grieving and quenching the Spirit is not a matter of minor consequence. The Word does not leave us with that option. God clearly shows us that grieving the Holy Spirit is a major issue with God Himself. In fact, He is heavily opposed to anyone grieving or quenching the Spirit as shown by His response to the Israelites when they did it in the Old Testament:

Isaiah 63:10
But [the Israelites] rebelled and grieved His Holy Spirit; so He turned Himself against them as an enemy, and He fought against them.

Also, in the New Testament it says:

James 4:4
Whosoever therefore will be a friend of the world is the enemy of God.

Grieving the Holy Spirit is tantamount to declaring war against a God you cannot fight. The Israelites tried it and the Word of God says that God "**turned Himself against them as an *enemy*, and He fought against them.**"

Now I'm sure you don't want to be on the wrong side of God; so it is of great importance for you as an heir to learn how to cooperate with the Holy Spirit and flee from grieving or quenching

Him. When we quench Him, we deny God the opportunity to bless and touch our lives and to touch the lives of others through us, for the Holy Spirit is God.

Notice what the scripture said in Acts 5 when Ananias and Sapphira lied:

Acts 5:3, 4
Why has Satan filled your heart to lie to the Holy Spirit... You have not lied to men but to God.

When someone grieves and quenches the Spirit, they have grieved and quenched God Himself, for the Lord is that Spirit. Ananias and Sapphira had grieved the Spirit of God by blatantly lying to the man of God, and like many today, they never even gave the matter a second thought when they decided to do it. They were not mindful of this very issue to which I am trying to direct your attention. They grieved the Spirit of God.

It is important to realise that you can never learn how not to quench Him until you give Him His proper place as God and not treat Him like an 'it' which some are doing to their peril. The Word of God says:

Acts 17:29-30
Forasmuch then as we are the offspring of God, we ought not to think that the Godhead is like unto gold, or silver, or stone, graven by art and man's device. And the times of this ignorance God winked at; but now commandeth all men everywhere to repent.

When we as the offspring of God start to classify the three manifestations of God like we do gold, silver, and stone, with levels of importance as if there is a separation between these manifestations, we will be messing it all up. This ignorance of

Hello Holy Spirit

treating the Holy Spirit as an 'it' God overlooked, but now He commands men everywhere to repent. It is no longer a case for discussion. It is a must. We should run away from thinking Jesus is simply a lesser God, and that the Holy Spirit is a wind lesser than God the Father and the Son for this is disobedience. These three are manifestations of the same God, hence Apostle Paul says:

2 Corinthians 3:17
The Lord is that Spirit.

In Psalm 95 you see praises being offered unto the "LORD," and it goes on to praise who He is. But when you read Hebrews 3:7-11, wherever Psalm 95 uses "LORD," Apostle Paul uses "the Holy Spirit" showing you who the Holy Spirit is. See!

Once this truth that the Holy Spirit is God penetrates our spirits, not only will we want to surrender to Him, but we will also stand in awe of His will which is to make His abode in us. When this happens, everything He says becomes important because all of a sudden, He is transformed in our thinking from a thing to a person. Then we will start thinking about how we can cooperate with Him rather than quench Him.

The Revelation

Apostle Paul said:

1 Thessalonians 5:19
Do not quench the Holy Spirit.

You will notice that this verse is simply one sentence and offers no explanation for what causes this quenching. That scripture only becomes clear when one begins to get a revelation that verse 19, "do not quench the Holy Spirit," is a conclusive emphasis of the instructions already given in verses 12-18 and 20-22.

The Holy Spirit in My Room!

Verse 19, "quench not the Spirit," is the main verse or if you will, the central commandment in 1 Thessalonians 5:12-22. All the other verses (12-18 and 20-22) are auxiliary. To put it another way, verse 19 is the commandment, and verses 12-18 and 20-22 are the explanations of the commandment. Therefore, if one does not follow verses 12-18 and 20-22, they will not understand how to obey the commandment in verse 19; consequently, they will have quenched the Spirit of God.

If we want to make it spiritually, or whichever way there is to make it, we ought to follow the mandate in verse 19, "do not quench the Holy Spirit." Your life depends on it. Therefore, it is necessary for us to thoroughly examine the surrounding verses to see how the Holy Spirit Himself defines quenching the Spirit. When we understand His definition, only then can we know how not to quench Him.

Fellowshipping with the Spirit

While the Lord has a lot to teach along this line, you must come to this knowledge that there is an important lesson on knowing how to fellowship with the Spirit first even before we get to 1 Thessalonians 5:12-22. After discussing fellowshipping with the Holy Spirit in the next chapter, we will start looking at verses 12-22 in greater depth. In doing so, we will explain further what we ought to do or ought not to do to keep the fire of the Holy Spirit burning so that we will be used mightily in miracles, signs, and wonders. Above all, we will walk with the Holy Spirit in the light of our Lord Jesus Christ and win many for Christ.

CHAPTER TWO

Fellowshipping with the Holy Spirit

That October afternoon the Holy Spirit taught me that living a supernatural life filled with miracles, signs, wonders, and demonstrations of God's power starts with knowing how not to quench the Spirit of God. On that day the Holy Spirit entered my room, words fail me to describe the emotions and thoughts that were surging through my mind. What had begun as just another quiet day, had just turned into the most extraordinary visitation of my life.

Now I need you to understand that I am a prophet. Seeing angels and visions are not new to me. But that moment when He stepped into my room was like nothing I had ever experienced in my entire life. I could not move, not because I was being restrained, but it seemed as if my physical body just did not know how to respond to this awesome presence. It was as if the walls in my room were standing at attention like they knew what was happening and who had just come into the room.

I was sitting there, and the whole room was filled with what I can only begin to describe as bright liquid white light. It was not a blinding light, yet it was so dense I couldn't see my hand if I put it in front of me. I felt like I was enveloped in love. I have never known anything like it! The scripture that says that God is love really came alive to me that day. Before I could wrap my head around what was happening, I watched as that light began to come together and formed a human-shaped being that sat in the sofa opposite me and said, "I am the Holy Spirit."

Fellowshipping with the Holy Spirit

When I say like a human-shaped form, I mean He had hands, legs, I could even have measured how tall he was (not that I did, but you get what I mean). One thing I have learnt to do is always to try and see whether each vision or visitation is consistent with what the Word of God says. No matter how good and exciting, if it is of God, it has to be consistent with scripture.

I sat there looking at this being who had just introduced Himself to me as the Holy Ghost. Now I know and have even taught that the Holy Spirit is a Person, and you cannot refer to Him as "it." But I tell you this was a shock to my system. I'm sitting there thinking *you have hands and legs like us*. I honestly don't know what I expected to see, but I got more than what I had bargained for. I know what I am describing to you right now is difficult for many to comprehend because you have always thought He was like wind; you never knew He was an actual Person.

I could sense His love, and it was overwhelming. I wanted to hug Him, but I wasn't sure if I could touch Him. I could scarcely believe He was right there staring at me in the face.

Who is the Holy Ghost?

I had a million questions racing through my mind. This experience was new and unusual, yet there was something that made me feel as if we already knew each other. I tried to think of Bible verses where anyone else had the same experience, and none were coming to mind. I had not even uttered a single word, but I could tell my mind was like an open book to Him. Before I could ask the question, He said to me, "Open Isaiah 63:9."

Isaiah 63:9
In all their affliction He was afflicted, and the Angel of His presence saved them: in His love and in His pity He redeemed them; and He bare them, and carried them all the days of old.

When I finished reading He said, "I am the Angel of God's presence." See, I had never thought about this when I read that scripture. You may not have either. But remember the Bible was written without punctuation. It was something that the translators of King James added so it would all make sense to us as we read.

Now, when you read that scripture, it tells us that the Angel of His Presence delivered them. Then the very next verse says, "they rebelled and vexed His Holy Spirit." That lets us know that the two terms "Angel of His Presence" and "Holy Spirit" are used interchangeably. We could have read it this way, "In all their affliction he was afflicted, and the Angel of His Presence saved them; and He bare them, and carried them all the days old. But they rebelled, and vexed the *Angel of His Presence*: therefore He was turned to be their enemy, and He fought against them." Are you getting it now?

That is why the scripture says He proceeds from the Father. He is the very manifestation of the presence of the Father. Let's read it together from the book of John.

John 15:26
But when the Comforter is come, whom I will send unto you from the Father, even the Spirit of truth, which proceedeth from the Father, He shall testify of Me.

The Holy Spirit hails from the Father, and when He comes, He is the very presence of the Father from whom He has emerged. Think about this. According to the Bible, Papa God has never left His throne in Heaven for anything, but you can be in your room praying and still sense His presence. How? It is because of the Holy Spirit. He proceeds from the Father and conveys the very presence of God to you.

Fellowshipping with the Holy Spirit

Notice in the first part of the scripture we have just read, the Lord Jesus says, "**whom I will send unto you from the Father**." From where will He send Him? He comes out of the Father and right there in your house becomes the presence of the same God who is still sitting on the throne.

You might be wondering how it is possible for Him to be simultaneously here with me and in your house on the other side of the world. Let me illustrate it this way. If I wanted to, right now I can video conference with five different people on different continents using just my phone. My voice and image will be just as clear as if they were here with me. Now if you and I can produce that kind of technology, what do you think God is able to do? Of course He can be in many different places at once!

As the Holy Spirit and I continued our conversation, I had so many questions racing through my mind I wasn't even sure where to start. I waited and listened because I knew the purpose for His visitation was greater than my mind could fathom.

It must be remembered that the Holy Spirit is the third Person of the Godhead. The biggest problem is many don't comprehend what that means. Some think of Him as the junior part of the Godhead, but nothing could be further from the truth. The Holy Spirit is not smaller than the Father or Jesus. Remember, if He is the Angel of God's presence that means that He is God. The presence of God cannot be inferior to the God whom it represents; it is all of God.

I know that might sound confusing, but you will get it in a minute as we discuss this next point. The Lord Jesus called the Holy Spirit His Father. The scripture says:

Hello Holy Spirit

John 14:10
Believest thou not that I am in the Father, and the Father in Me? The words that I speak unto you I speak not of Myself: but the Father that dwelleth in Me, He doeth the works.

This statement confused even the Pharisees that were listening to the Lord Jesus. They did not know He was referring to the Holy Spirit. When He said "the Father in Me," He was actually talking about the Spirit of God in Him and called Him His Father. I know this is a difficult one to swallow for most so let's go a bit deeper into the Word. Watch what the scripture says:

Luke 1:35
And the angel answered and said unto her, The Holy Ghost shall come upon thee, and the power of the Highest shall overshadow thee: therefore also that holy thing which shall be born of thee shall be called the Son of God.

The scripture is telling us that Jesus was conceived by the Holy Ghost, so there is definitely no way that He can be the junior part of the Godhead. He is the Father of Jesus. So, when the Lord referred to the Father in Him in John 14:10, He was speaking of the Holy Ghost; He is the One who conceived Him and was living on the inside of Him.

I know I have just messed up your theology right there, but this stuff is in your Bible. When you study the Bible, you will find that the Lord Jesus would refer to both the Father in Heaven and the Father in Him. We know from the book of Genesis that God the Father has ceased from His work and is resting; He has not moved from his heavenly throne since the beginning of creation. His presence by the Spirit of God allows us to fellowship with Him. This is simply amazing!

Luke 11:13
If ye then, being evil, know how to give good gifts unto your children: how much more shall your heavenly Father give the Holy Spirit to them that ask Him?

Now when the Lord Jesus refers in this passage to the heavenly Father, He is not talking about the Holy Spirit but to the person of the Father. The Spirit of God is the manifestation of God the Father's presence here on Earth. That is why the Lord Jesus could say of Him that He is just like the Father. Watch what the scripture says:

John 14:16-17a
And I will pray the Father, and He shall give you another Comforter, that He may abide with you for ever; even the Spirit of Truth; whom the world cannot receive, because it seeth Him not, neither knoweth Him: but ye know Him; for He dwelleth with you, and shall be in you.

Once more we see a distinction being made between the Father in Heaven and the Holy Spirit, the Father in Him. In this passage, the word 'another' is the Greek word *allos* which translates literally as 'another of the same kind.' The Lord Jesus was telling His followers that the Holy Spirit who was coming would be like Him in the sense that He brings and manifests the presence of the Father. That is why when Philip the disciple of the Lord asked to see the Father, the Lord's response was shocking to them at the time. Let's see what the scripture says:

John 14:8-9
Philip saith unto Him, Lord, show us the Father, and it sufficeth us. Jesus saith unto Him, Have I been so long time with you, and yet hast thou not known Me, Philip? He that hath seen Me hath seen the Father; and how sayest thou then, Show us the Father?

I need you to understand that Philip was asking to see the Father here, and the Lord Jesus turns around to him and says you are looking at Father. Think about it. The Lord Jesus is the express image of the Father. In other words, He is the precise reproduction of God the Father.

Hebrews 1:3
Who being the brightness of His glory, and the express image of His person, and upholding all things by the word of His power, when He had by Himself purged our sins, sat down on the right hand of the Majesty on high.

The Greek term translated as 'image' in the passage in Hebrews refers to a template that can be used to reproduce a coin. When the coin is melted and poured into the template, it comes out in the exact image of that template.

The Lord Jesus and the Holy Spirit are the same in that they both manifest who God the Father is to us. This should put to rest the erroneous belief that the Holy Spirit is the lesser part of the Godhead. In reality, He is the very presence of the Father.

The Holy Spirit in the Godhead

The Holy Spirit is the third person of the Godhead, and He is the conveyer of the presence and the power of God. The scripture we read earlier in the book of Isaiah calls Him the "Angel" of God's presence.

Isaiah 63:9-10
In all their affliction He was afflicted, and the Angel of His Presence saved them: in His love and in His pity He redeemed them; and He bare them, and carried them all the days of old. But they rebelled, and vexed His holy Spirit: therefore He was turned to be their enemy, and He fought against them.

That means He is the messenger of God's presence, yet He is so independent of the Father from whom He came. He is the one who helps you enjoy spiritual things. He can be in you fully as though you are the only one on earth, and still be ministering to someone on the other side of the world.

Paul prayed the Ephesians would be filled with all the fullness of God. How is that even possible? If you pray and God answers that prayer, that means you now have all of Him in you.

Ephesians 3:19
And to know the love of Christ, which passeth knowledge, that ye might be filled with all the fullness of God.

That is the ministry of the Holy Ghost. Remember, He is the Spirit of God. He proceeds from the Father, and He is in you and in me as though He is nowhere else. You don't have a part of Him; you have all of Him with His awesome ability. What manner of person are you meant to be? You have been brought into absolute mastery. You have been given more power than you will ever need in the Holy Spirit. You only need to awaken to the reality of His Person.

The Spirit Upon and the Spirit Within

The reason why most of the Church demonstrate very little or no power these days is they are missing the pillar of it all, the Holy Spirit. The Lord Jesus made a most remarkable statement which, although it is scripture, has been realised in the lives of very few in the Church today. We find it in John's account:

John 14:12
Verily, verily, I say unto you, He that believeth on Me, the works that I do shall he do also; and greater works than these shall he do; because I go unto My Father.

That is absolutely mind-blowing! Many of you have picked up this book because you are christians and that is your confession. In fact, if I went to Africa today, the majority of the people there are christians. I could pick up a stone and throw it at a crowd of people at the market, and ninety percent of the time it will hit a christian. Notwithstanding, it is virtually impossible to find someone who can perform the miracles that the Lord Jesus used to do let alone greater works.

I know I have many witnesses right now, and we have to get to the bottom of this. Either the Lord Jesus lied to us, or we are missing something in what He said. Notice He did not say the prophets or the bishops who believe in Him will do greater works, no! That Bible verse was written for every christian on Earth, yet here we are with no greater works to talk about. This is what the Lord began to teach me that day He walked into my room.

The key to the answer to this problem is in that very same verse we just read. The Lord Jesus said, "and greater works than these shall he do; because I go unto my Father." What many forget is what He had told His disciples was going to happen when He went to the Father. Watch what the scripture says:

John 16:7
Nevertheless I tell you the truth; It is expedient for you that I go away: for if I go not away, the Comforter will not come unto you; but if I depart, I will send Him unto you.

The Lord Jesus is declaring the reason they can do greater works. He says when I'm with the Father, the Holy Spirit who is working in Me to do all these miracles will now be in you. Hallelujah! Think about it. It would be unfair for the Lord Jesus to expect us to do what He did and even more if we do not have what enabled Him. In fact, it would be evil! Many are without power simply because they are strangers to the Holy Ghost even though He is there for each of us. He is a companion for life, but many never give a second thought to what might grieve Him.

In the scripture we read earlier, the Lord pointed us to the Holy Spirit as the source of all the miracles He was doing in His earthly ministry. He attributed even the wisdom of His teaching to the Holy Spirit. Let's look at it again:

John 14:10
Believest thou not that I am in the Father, and the Father in Me? The words that I speak unto you I speak not of Myself: but the Father that dwelleth in Me, He doeth the works.

He said, "I speak not of Myself." If that was the case, who was telling Him what to say? The Holy Spirit of course! He is the power of God. Even the apostle Paul caught this revelation when He wrote to the Corinthians:

1 Corinthians 2:4
And my speech and my preaching was not with enticing words of man's wisdom, but in demonstration of the Spirit and of power.

Paul was merely telling them he had not learnt the things He was preaching from the cemetery, sorry seminary. He was preaching the Word inspired by the Holy Ghost Himself. That is where the power is, brother!

I recall an occasion when I was ministering in Harare, Zimbabwe, in 2012. It was an open-air service. An enormous crowd had gathered, and I began preaching. Halfway through the sermon, I saw storm clouds gathering. It was inevitably going to rain, but I did not have that release from the Lord to stop the service. Suddenly it started raining heavily, and I found myself pointing to the clouds and commanded the rain to stop. As quickly as it had begun, the rain stopped, and I could see the sunshine breaking through the clouds.

You need to understand that when I did that, it was not something I had planned to do before I left home that day. In fact, I was just as shocked as everybody else to hear those word coming out of my mouth. My mind had no time to process the whole thing.
The day the Lord came into my room, He explained to me that because I was preaching the Word as the Lord had given it to me, it was easy for Him to use me to stop the rain that was about to stop the entire service. There is a certain boldness that comes over you when you are full of the Holy Ghost. The things that normally move you become nonentities. This is exactly what happened to the disciples in the book of Acts:

Acts 4:31
And when they had prayed, the place was shaken where they were assembled together; and they were all filled with the Holy Ghost, and they spake the word of God with boldness.

These are the same men who ran for dear life and deserted the Lord Jesus at His arrest. Now they were preaching the Gospel with boldness. What changed? The only that had changed was that they were now full of the Holy Ghost! The more you get to know this wonderful Holy Spirit, the same thing that happened to them will happen to you!

Brothers and sisters, we are just getting warmed up. I have much more to share with you, so stay with me as we get into this next chapter. My prayer for you is that as you read the words in this book the revelation contained therein will become your reality.

CHAPTER THREE

The Holy Spirit in Christ

What I am about to tell you will probably contradict everything you were taught since Sunday school, so I thought it wise to prepare you for it. If you are standing, please sit. You would have heard from many preachers how the Lord Jesus said, "The Spirit of the Lord is upon Me." Well, that's not actually what He said, and I will prove it to you from your very own Bible. *Yes Prophet, but what about Luke 4:18?* I hear you, so let's start from there. I am going to back up a little so we can get the full context of what we are reading here.

Luke 4:16-21
And He came to Nazareth, where He had been brought up: and, as His custom was, He went into the synagogue on the sabbath day, and stood up for to read. And there was delivered unto Him the book of the prophet Esaias. And when He had opened the book, He found the place where it was written, "The Spirit of the Lord is upon me, because he hath anointed me to preach the gospel to the poor; he hath sent me to heal the brokenhearted, to preach deliverance to the captives, and recovering of sight to the blind, to set at liberty them that are bruised, to preach the acceptable year of the Lord." And He closed the book, and He gave it again to the minister, and sat down. And the eyes of all them that were in the synagogue were fastened on Him. And He began to say unto them, "This day is this scripture fulfilled in your ears."

The Bible is telling us here that Jesus had come into the temple, as was His custom. They gave Him the book of the prophet Isaiah where He found the place where it was written, "The Spirit of the Lord is upon me." It is important to realize that the words Jesus is reading here are the words of Isaiah, not His own. There was a limitation in the choice of words that Isaiah used because of the revelation of the Spirit of God that they had in the Old Testament. Let me explain.

When you look at the account of everyone that was used by God in the Old Testament, the Bible records that the Spirit of the Lord came upon them. Then they would prophesy or do whatever task for which they were anointed. They only knew the Spirit upon but were never filled with the Holy Ghost. That is why when God was communicating the words of that prophecy to Isaiah, He could use only what Isaiah knew—the Spirit upon. The whole concept of being filled with the Spirit was alien to Isaiah.

There are many things that we enjoy today as New Testament christians that folks who lived in the Old Testament never dreamt of seeing. Jesus Himself said:

Matthew 13:17
For verily I say unto you, that many prophets and righteous men have desired to see those things which ye see, and have not seen them; and to hear those things which ye hear, and have not heard them.

They did not have the full revelation of what salvation entails for the New Testament christian. Even the audience of Jesus had no idea what He was trying to say to them when He read that passage in Luke 4. Jesus did not merely have the Spirit upon Him; He was filled with the Spirit, but that was unfathomable in those days. Watch what the scripture says:

The Holy Spirit in Christ

Luke 4:1
And Jesus being full of the Holy Ghost returned from Jordan and was led by the Spirit into the wilderness.

Before we even get to the part in verse 18 where it says, "The Spirit of the Lord is upon me," the Bible already tells us in verse 1 that Jesus was "full of the Holy Ghost." He had more than the Spirit upon. Are you getting it?

Let me ask you this, what made John the Baptist the greatest of all who were in the Old Testament? Remember, this is what the Lord Jesus said. Let's look at that passage:

Matthew 11:11
Verily I say unto you, among them that are born of women there hath not risen a greater than John the Baptist: notwithstanding he that is least in the kingdom of heaven is greater than he.

That passage in most Bibles is printed in red indicating that it is the Lord Jesus speaking. But what would really make John greater than Moses who parted the red sea, or Elijah who killed the prophets of Baal, or Samuel of whom it is recorded that no word he spoke ever fell to the ground? Since the Bible says that the one who is least in the Kingdom of God is greater than John, that means you are greater than John, even greater than Abraham, the Father of Faith. What entitles you to hold that position?

Luke 1:14-15
And thou shalt have joy and gladness; and many shall rejoice at his birth. For he shall be great in the sight of the Lord, and shall drink neither wine nor strong drink; and he shall be filled with the Holy Ghost, even from his mother's womb.

You see, John the Baptist is the only person other than Jesus that the scripture records as having been filled with the Spirit in the

Old Testament. That was enough to set him apart from everyone else. In the same way, you and I as New Testament christians today are considered to be greater than all the mighty men of valour that lived under the old testament. John was filled with the Spirit from his mother's womb, and when you got born again, the same Holy Spirit came to live on the inside of you.

2 Corinthians 4:7
But we have this treasure in earthen vessels, that the excellency of the power may be of God, and not of us.

The treasure of which Paul spoke about here is the Holy Spirit! Hallelujah! He is the reason why the Lord Jesus would call you greater than John. He has made Himself one with you.

The Lord reminded me of one particular service in the city of Manchester in the UK where I was ministering in the prophetic and a demon began to manifest. This dear sister was clearly tormented by this evil spirit. I remember commanding the evil spirit to get off the floor in the Name of Jesus. When she stood before me, she could not look at my eyes. It was as if they were a source of pain or something. Now I have looked at myself in the mirror many times and to me, my eyes look just the same as anybody else's. But this demon was seeing different. The Lord said to me, "It wasn't your eyes the demon was afraid of, it was Mine."

This is another of many examples I could give to show the extraordinary power of this remarkable Person, the Holy Spirit. As you can see, there is nothing "junior" about Him. The reason why many in the Body of Christ today consider Him to be the lesser part of the Godhead is that He is the last to be revealed to us. When you look at the Old Testament, you find that even though He is there when creation is being birthed, the saints of old did not have a relationship with Him as we do. The first mention of the Spirit is in the very first chapter of the book of Genesis.

Genesis 1:2
And the earth was without form, and void; and darkness was upon the face of the deep. And the Spirit of God moved upon the face of the waters.

That Hebrew word translated as 'moved' in that passage is *rachaph*, and it means 'to flutter in constant imagination.' The Holy Spirit is the power of God that was bringing everything that was being spoken by God into existence. That is why the Lord Jesus said the Father who dwells in Me, He is the one that doeth the works.

John 14:10
Believest thou not that I am in the Father, and the Father in Me? The words that I speak unto you I speak not of Myself: but the Father that dwelleth in Me, He doeth the works.

Remember, Jesus is referring to the Father in Him, not the Father in Heaven; so we know He is talking about the Spirit of God. In the Old Testament, they never knew Him. It is only after the death and resurrection of the Lord that He came to live in christians.

The Old Testament saints were anointed for service, and the Spirit of God would come upon them to perform a particular function. For instance, kings were anointed to rule, and prophets were anointed in their service and office. The Spirit of God would come upon them to prophesy and do whatever the Lord would be leading them to do.

Judges 6:34
So the Spirit of the Lord came upon Gideon; and he blew a trumpet, and the Abiezrites were called together to follow him.

1 Samuel 16:13 NASB
Then Samuel took the horn of oil and anointed him in the midst of his brothers; and the Spirit of the Lord came mightily upon David from that day forward.

I could quote many other scriptures that the Lord began to show me. In the Old Testament, they did not know Him as we do in the New Testament. He could not come to live inside of them as the Lord Jesus told His disciples He would.

John 14:16-17
And I will pray the Father, and He shall give you another Comforter, that He may abide with you for ever; even the Spirit of truth; whom the world cannot receive, because it seeth Him not, neither knoweth Him: but ye know Him; for He dwelleth with you, and shall be in you.

When you are born again, the Holy Spirit comes to live on the inside of you and makes His home in you. He is that Friend that sticks closer than a brother. He empowers you, and His presence in your life changes everything. The difference between you and a non-christian is His presence in your life. Your body has become His temple. Where you go, He goes, which is why it is crucial for every christian to know how to cooperate with and not grieve the Spirit of God.

Baptised in the Holy Spirit

Even though the Holy Spirit wants to do all these wonderful things with you and is full of power, you will die like a mere man as long as you are ignorant of who He is and how not to quench and frustrate Him. The Bible says My people perish for the lack of knowledge. Even in the early Church some christians knew nothing of the Holy Spirit and went about their business as if they were

Old Testament christians. When the apostle Paul came to Ephesus, he met a few christians in this exact position.

Acts 19:1-2
And it came to pass, that, while Apollos was at Corinth, Paul having passed through the upper coasts came to Ephesus: and finding certain disciples, he said unto them, Have ye received the Holy Ghost since ye believed? And they said unto him, We have not so much as heard whether there be any Holy Ghost.

These were bona fide christians; the scripture even calls them disciples. That means that they had the Holy Spirit living on the inside of them, and yet they had no idea of the power they carried—not even an awareness—until Paul got there. Watch what happened:

Acts 19:6
And when Paul had laid his hands upon them, the Holy Ghost came on them; and they spake with tongues, and prophesied.

Hallelujah! Right now even as you are going through the pages of this book, there is an awakening on the inside of you, a stirring. That revelation is becoming your reality.

Now, I want you to notice that the Bible says the Holy Ghost came "on" them. He was already inside, but what they had not yet experienced was the baptism which is what enables you to do the mighty works. As soon as they received, they were speaking in tongues and prophesying. The Spirit of God overshadowed them. What happened to them was exactly what happened to Mary when she conceived the Lord. The Bible puts it this way:

Luke 1:35
And the angel answered and said unto her, The Holy Ghost shall come upon thee, and the power of the Highest shall overshadow

thee: therefore also that holy thing which shall be born of thee shall be called the Son of God.

Mary's overshadowing by the Holy Ghost is the same experience that every christians has when they are baptised in the Holy Spirit. He wants to commune with you. It is a grave mistake that christians have failed to understand that the Holy Spirit longs and yearns for our friendship. The Holy Spirit wants to be treated like a friend. He wants to speak to us and hear us speak to Him, to laugh with us. He longs for our fellowship. That is why the Apostle Paul wrote:

2 Corinthians 13:14
The grace of the Lord Jesus Christ, and the love of God, and the communion of the Holy Spirit be with you all.

The word 'communion' here is rendered *koinōnía* in the Greek, meaning a close association between persons, emphasising what is common between them, and by extension, participation, sharing, contribution, and communication. The friendship of the Holy Spirit is not only a relationship between a christian to another christian but between the person and the Holy Spirit. The extension of this word *koinōnía* is very clear and conveys a lot about the deep friendship that He wants to have with us.

The extension of the word *koinōnía* is *koinonikos* which refers to a willingness to share and a willingness to communicate. This lets us know that the Holy Spirit is very willing to communicate and share with us. He longs for a close relationship full of communication and reciprocal sharing where people share their heart with Him, and He likewise shares His truth with us.

Many people mistakenly think what Apostle Paul said in 2 Corinthians 13:14 was referring to christians communicating with each other in the Spirit. But he was talking about the beautiful and sweet fellowship the Holy Spirit longs to have with every one of us. That is why he says, "the communion of the Holy Spirit be with you all."

You see, the Holy Spirit communes with our spirits. The Bible tells us that:

Romans 8:16
The Spirit Himself testifies with our spirit that we are God's children.

He speaks from within. It is a fellowship of the spirit, and this privilege is given only to those who are God's children. When you understand that the Holy Spirit was given to fellowship with you, only then will you start realising that in any sweet fellowship there are no petitions or requests as there are in prayer. In fellowship we do things together. In prayer, I pray for the food that we eat to be blessed, and I thank God for His provision. But in a sweet fellowship, I ask the Holy Spirit to join me for breakfast.

The Holy Spirit Is Not an Errand Boy

In fellowship, the Holy Spirit wants to be involved. He is not an errand boy. He is here to help and to stand by us. When we know this and work on our relationship with the Holy Spirit, miracles, signs, and wonders can't help themselves but show up. His power becomes our power. His supernatural abilities become ours.

One day, I simply told the Holy Spirit that I was inviting Him to a conference call I was having with one of my branches in Africa. He was glad to join me, and I was absolutely delighted to have Him. I preached over the phone with the help of the Holy Spirit. After just a few minutes on the call, I heard the pastor say to me, "Can you stop preaching for a while?" I asked why and to my surprise, the pastor answered, "There's no one listening. The power of God came like a wind into the room, and everyone fell under the power of the Holy Spirit!" Many with sicknesses were healed of their diseases, and their pains disappeared! Why did it happen like that? My Friend, the Holy Spirit, had released His presence on the people. He didn't care if we were on the phone or using a tin can telephone. He was invited to the phone call and boy, did He show up!

The Holy Spirit Our Helper

In prayer you go before God to pray for many things. But in the fellowship with the Holy Spirit, the Holy Ghost will tell you to invite Him so He can help you pray. That is what Apostle Paul was saying in the book of Romans:

Romans 8:26-27
Likewise the Spirit also helps in our weaknesses. For we do not know what we should pray for as we ought, but the Spirit Himself makes intercession for us with groanings which cannot be uttered.

Did you notice the phrases "helps in our weaknesses" and "makes intercession for us with groanings?" They are an indication that the Holy Spirit is a helper here. We are not praying to Him. He is groaning while helping us pray. We are having a sweet fellowship where He props us up in our problems and helps us pray the will of God upon our lives.

The Holy Spirit's fellowship is that of a close friendship where I invite Him to whatever I am doing so He can offer guidance. When I develop this kind of relationship where I see the Holy Spirit as the Helper, then I am on the right path to knowing how not to grieve the Holy Spirit or quench Him. Consider this. If you have a friend, you would want to know how he feels, what his interests are, what his hobbies are, or what he likes to hear. Well, the same is true with the Holy Spirit. He is a Friend. christians need to embrace the friendship of the Holy Spirit. Our relationship with Him should be so intimate that we sit down to lunch with Him, ask how He is, tell Him goodnight when we sleep, and even good morning when we wake up.

Living a supernatural life filled with miracles, signs, wonders and demonstrations of God's power must be driven by two things: our desire to know the Holy Spirit at a personal level and allowing Him to teach what He needs and wants us to do with Him. This is so crucial and wonderful!

The Holy Spirit and His Emotions

We understand that the Holy Spirit has all the qualities that we typically associate with people. We enter into a relationship with Him in a similar manner to the way we enter into relationships with other people. He is not just a blind, unfeeling, unintelligent force. The fact that He does not have a physical body (like ours) presents most of us with a problem. In our thinking, a person usually lives in a body. But the Holy Spirit is spirit, as is God the Father, and doesn't have a material body so to speak. We have to remember He lives in a different dimension than that with which we are familiar. Jesus is easier for us to understand because He entered into our human experience which involved sharing human nature and a human body. Obviously, He is a person. But as we explore the New Testament, we also find that the Holy Spirit is constantly spoken of in personal terms.

The Word of God clearly shows that the Holy Spirit is a Person. He *speaks* God's message (Acts 28:25-27), *bears witness* together with our own spirits (Romans 8:16), *helps* us in our weakness (Romans 8:26), *convicts* people of guilt and judgment (John 16:8), *guides*

God's people (John 16:13), *tells* us things that are to come (John 16:13), *brings glory* to Jesus (John 16:14), *hears* God's truths and *makes them known* (John 16:13, 15), *intercedes* on our behalf (Romans 8:26, 27), *searches* all things (1 Corinthians 2:10), *knows* the mind of God (1 Corinthians 2:11), *teaches* the content of the Gospel to christians (1 Corinthians 2:13), *lives* among and within christians (1 Corinthians 3:16; John 14:16, 16:7), *washes, sanctifies,* and *justifies* God's people (1 Corinthians 6:11), *gives* gifts to His people as He determines (1 Corinthians 12:11), *gives life* to those who believe (2 Corinthians 3:6).

The Holy Spirit *cries out* from within our hearts (Galatians 4:6), *leads* us in the ways of God (Galatians 5:18), *has desires* that are in opposition to the flesh (Galatians 5:17), *strengthens* christians (Ephesians 3:16), *is grieved* by our sinfulness (Ephesians 4:30), can be *blasphemed* (Luke 12:10) and *lied to* (Acts 5:3). He is a Person who yearns for a relationship just as you yearn for a relationship. He longs to have a relationship with christians. He wants to talk and discuss with you. He is willing to communicate, so give Him time and see how you will surprise those around you with the power of God.

Upsetting the Fellowship with the Holy Spirit

I remember a time when the prophetic unction became so open to the public. I called out names that I had no idea of or had never heard before; I mentioned specific details of people's lives that I had no way of knowing. When I did, I only ended at the blessings that those individuals I called out were going to receive. I left out the bad habits that the Holy Spirit had revealed were in these people's lives, and that grieved Him very much. Though I didn't realize it at the time, I was in disobedience big time! See, I had all the verses like Romans 2:4 (the goodness of God turns people to repentance) to justify my actions. The people were smiling, but the Holy Spirit was not! He wanted me to correct the bad and sinful areas of those people's lives that were affecting their relationship with Him. But I was so hung up on the blessing, I had ignored rebuking sin.

This mistake showed me yet another wonderful side of the Holy Spirit. He was not trying to expose and humiliate people but was more focused on getting His relationship with these people fixed. He wanted the rebuke intact so that His relationship with the people I was prophesying to would be a great one. He brings conviction not condemnation, and there is a big difference between the two. Conviction will make you run to God because you realise how much what you have done grieves Him and you want to make it right. Condemnation, on the other hand, causes you to run away from God and feel unworthy of His love. The Holy Spirit is there to reveal to you the goodness of God and lead you into the best that God intended for you.

It Is a Must

Jesus said the disciples would be better off with the presence of the Holy Spirit in their lives than they were with His company while He was with them on earth (John 16:7). That means the Holy Spirit must at least have the personal qualities that Jesus possessed. It also means fellowship with the Spirit is a must for He gives us the greatest advantage.

John 16:7 NASB
It is to your advantage that I go away; for if I do not go away, the Helper will not come to you.

This is astounding! Jesus says it is better for Him to go and leave the disciples with the Holy Spirit. One can't help but wonder what quality the Holy Spirit possesses that Jesus doesn't for Him to make such an astonishing statement. Then in another place He says:

John 14:28
Ye have heard how I said unto you, I go away, and come again unto you. If ye loved Me, ye would rejoice, because I said, I go unto the Father: for My Father is greater than I.

This is something that is so misunderstood by many christians. Here we see the Godhead in action and the manifestation of God's functions in His triune nature. Jesus says I am going, and the Holy Spirit cannot come if I am still here. Why? It is simple. This is just a mystery of God having three manifestations. Jesus is saying it is an advantage to have this fellowship with the Holy Spirit because it is that manifestation that is capable of having deep fellowship. Knowing this, we ought to make the most of our relationship with the Holy Spirit.

When the Holy Spirit came into the lives of the disciples their language changed. They started proclaiming that they were witnesses with the Spirit. They were including the Holy Spirit in what they were saying. The Holy Spirit became the Companion with whom they witnessed and talked to the people. The disciples were now power-packed, and the Spirit of God had become their Friend. I know firsthand the transforming power of this Friend we call the Holy Spirit and how that power changes things. Cancers, tumours, wheelchair-bound people, diabetes, and many other ailments have been healed through my hands by this sweet Holy Spirit. He will do the same for anyone who will listen and fellowship with Him. He is a dear Friend, and without Him, nothing will get people this free.

He is our Friend, and surely if you have a friend, you would want to know how he feels, what his interests are, what his hobbies are, or

The Holy Spirit in Christ

what he likes to hear. The same is true of the Holy Spirit. He is a Friend, and more so, the Lord Jesus Christ said it is an advantage to have Him as a Helper. We ought to get that sorted out, so we can have His abilities to be ours; His power to be our power; His love for us to be our love for those that are around us and also for Him.

Supernatural Fellowship in My Life

Not long after starting Spirit Embassy and Royal Tower in the UK, I ventured out with a few people in the evangelism arm of the ministry. We would go out and try to win the lost. I say "try" because all I was doing was an attempt, not supernatural power evangelism. Then one day when I realised all this dawdling and dithering was not taking me anywhere, I had a eureka moment, as it were; I asked the Holy Spirit to help me win souls.

I went into a certain Chinese restaurant with three of our church members and sat down to eat. As I sat there, the Holy Spirit told me to go and speak to a certain Chinese waitress in that restaurant. As I obeyed, the Holy Spirit told me her name, her boyfriend's name in China, her bank account balance, and the problems she was having all to her great surprise. Remember, this was happening in the UK and most of the details I disclosed by the fellowship of the Spirit were related to or in China. Only a few of the things the Holy Spirit revealed to me supernaturally were in the UK. After I told her all these things, the Holy Spirit told me to introduce Christ right in the middle of her surprise. With her mouth still wide open I went for it, and she listened as I told her of Christ's power. From that day forward, I started winning souls with the Holy Spirit. The supernatural became normal every time all because I had surrendered myself to the leading and friendship of the Holy Spirit. He is a Friend indeed!

The Fruit the Fellowship Produces

It is important that the "fruit" that the spirit of man produces through the fellowship of the Spirit be seen and known to be our personal qualities: "**love, joy, peace, patience, kindness, goodness, faithfulness, gentleness, and self-control**" (Galatians 5:22, 23). You see, this fruit is mainly personal qualities having to do with our relationships. They are also qualities often attributed to God in His relationship with us. A blind "force" or "influence" does not produce love!

We have the privilege of enjoying friendship with Him. Additionally, He creates friendship between christians. Ask Him how He feels, how He wants to be treated, and what He likes. Know His interests and His mind and learn His ways. Do everything with Him. Involve Him. That is the relationship. That is the fellowship that produces the fruit of the Spirit.

When I stand up to preach, I invite the Holy Spirit to preach with me and share His thoughts through me. When I do this, the preaching many times becomes prophetic with me calling out names of people and describing places where I have never been. I always see into the spiritual realms and know the hearts of men and women and what they have been doing without them telling me anything beforehand. Why is this possible? The answer is simple: the Holy Spirit who is my Friend and my Companion tells me all these things. He shares with me the secrets of people's hearts, and it's all because I know Him on a personal level and intimately.

I know that the Bible does use impersonal metaphors such as fire, breath, wind, and water. However, it is significant that Paul, who probably has more to say about the relationships that exist between the three manifestations of God than any other writer, tends to avoid such imagery. It's not because they are wrong to use, but Paul wants to concentrate more on the Holy Spirit as a Person rather than on just the metaphors that describe part of how He functions or what He can do. That is why he uses verbs of personal action that are used elsewhere of God and Christ.

Paul uses the Spirit, *Pneuma* in the Greek, as the masculine pronoun 'He,' giving Him identity. The Holy Spirit is portrayed as a personal being and is identified as "I" in Acts:

Acts 13:2
Separate Me Barnabas and Saul for the work whereunto I have called them.

The Holy Spirit here in Acts 13:2 refers to Himself as "I" signifying that the Spirit of God is a 'He' *not* an 'it.' Therefore, we ought to treat Him as such if we want to flow with the power of the Holy Spirit and not quench Him. Here it is even more significant because this is the Holy Spirit calling Himself a Person by saying "I." It is now established by the Holy Spirit Himself that He is a 'He.' It is no longer a theological argument. It has become a divine fact.

Flowing with the Power of the Spirit Through Fellowship

When the word 'quench' is used in Scripture, it is speaking of suppressing fire. When christians put on the shield of faith as part of their armour of God (Ephesians 6:16), they are suppressing the power of the fiery darts from Satan. Christ described hell as a place where the fire would not be "quenched" (Mark 9:44, 46, 48). Likewise, the Holy Spirit is a fire dwelling in each christians, and He wants to express Himself in our actions and attitudes. When we as christians do not allow the Spirit to be seen in our actions and attitudes, when we do what we know is wrong, we suppress or "quench" the Spirit. If we do not allow the Spirit to reveal Himself the way that He wants to, then we are already grieving Him.

Hello Holy Spirit

Only a person can be grieved. Therefore, it stands to reason that the Spirit must be a Person in order to experience this emotion. Once we appreciate this aspect, we can better understand how He is grieved, mainly because we too experience grief sometimes. Ephesians 4:30 tells us that we should not "grieve" the Spirit. Let's stay in the passage to understand what Paul is telling us. We can grieve the Spirit by living like the pagans (4:17-19), by yielding to our sin nature (4:22-24), by lying (4:25), by holding on to anger (4:26-27), by stealing (4:28), by cursing (4:29), by becoming bitter (4:31), by being unforgiving (4:32), by sexual immorality (5:3-5). To grieve the Spirit is to act out in a sinful manner, whether it is in thought and deed, or in thought only.

This agrees with the verses we began with in 1 Thessalonians 5:12-22:

12 And we beseech you, brethren, to *know them which labour among you, and are over you in the Lord*, and admonish you; 13 And to *esteem them very highly in love for their work's sake*. And *be at peace among yourselves*. 14 Now we exhort you, brethren, *warn them that are unruly, comfort the feebleminded, support the weak, be patient toward all men*. 15 *See that none render evil for evil unto any man; but ever follow that which is good, both among yourselves, and to all men*. 16 *Rejoice evermore*. 17 *Pray without ceasing*. 18 *In every thing give thanks: for this is the will of God in Christ Jesus concerning you*. 19 *Quench not the Spirit*. 20 *Despise not prophesyings*. 21 *Prove all things; hold fast that which is good*. 22 *Abstain from all appearance of evil*. [emphasis added]

Galatinas Revelation vs Thesalonians Revelation

Here is something you don't have to miss. You see every instruction in these verses in 1 Thessalonians 5:12-22 come under the umbrella of love. What Paul was actually teaching here, is the exact same thing he had written to the Galatian church when he was admonishing them to walk in the spirit. In fact, let's look at that scripture one more time;

Galations 5: 22- 24
Now the works of the flesh are manifest, which are these; Adultery, fornication, uncleanness, lasciviousness, Idolatry, witchcraft, hatred, variance, emulations, wrath, strife, seditions, heresies, Envyings, murders, drunkenness, revellings, and such like: of the which I tell you before, as I have also told you in time past, that they which do such things shall not inherit the kingdom of God. But the fruit of the Spirit is love, joy, peace, longsuffering, gentleness, goodness, faith, Meekness, temperance: against such there is no law.

Now we know that the works of the flesh that are described here certainly grieve and quench the Spirit of God, but then Paul points them to the FRUIT of the Spirit and as we go into this next chapter it will become even clearer that when he wrote to that letter to the Thessalonians he was simply giving them the practical side of what he had instructed the Galatians to do.

By paying attention to these passages and the instructions found therein, we can avoid grieving and consequently quenching the Holy Spirit's fire in our lives. This enables us to maintain our sweet fellowship with Him. This can only be done by walking in love. So, in each remaining chapter, I will show you a clear correlation between each of these instructions in 1 Thessalonians 5:12-22 and the fruit of the Spirit in Galatians 5:22-24 which is love. As we get into the next chapter, you will be as shocked as I was to discover what it is how not quenching the Spirit is tantamount walking in the Spirit which walking in love ad it will revolutionise your relationship with the Holy Spirit!

CHAPTER FOUR

Honouring Those Sent of God

The two-hour visitation by God the Holy Spirit up in the jutting moorlands of Barnby- in-the-Willows brought a fresh way of *koinōnia*, fellowship with Him. That afternoon the Holy Spirit visited me, He went straight to the first thing that would prevent Him from being quenched. He went directly to the first thing that makes Him not to be vexed, insulted, angered, snuffed out to the point He will retreat from speaking.

The first thing shocked me, not because I do not practice it, but because the Holy Spirit told me this was number one, in the sense of what is of chief importance. He said,

"Honour those that are sent and are above you in the Lord."

Notice here that this coincides with what Apostle Paul wrote to the Thessalonians under the influence of the same Holy Spirit who invaded my house that afternoon in October. The scripture says:

1 Thessalonians 5:12-13a
And we beseech you, brethren, to know them which labour among you, and are over you in the Lord, and admonish you; and to esteem them very highly in love.

Before we begin to dig into what this verse means, let me remind you of what I said in the previous chapter. Each instruction the Holy Spirit gave me that day is carried out by walking in some aspect of the fruit of the Spirit which is love. Knowing and esteeming highly those who are over you requires humility and meekness which is a component of the fruit of the Spirit.

The word 'meekness' comes from the word *praótēs* which is translated 'humility.' It carries with it the idea of being teachable while being submitted under someone in a higher or more knowledgeable position. When you look at the definition of the word meek you will find that it actually points to submissiveness. In order to show honour or even to acknowledge that someone is above in the things of God or anything else for that matter, calls for you to be meek. Imagine all these things Paul was teaching here are all encapsulated in the fruit of the Spirit, love.

Now remember when we talk about meekness this the exact same thing that Paul gave to the Galatians as an attribute of the fruit of the Spirit which is love, so then teaching to honour those above Paul was simply now giving them the practicalities of it all.

Galatians 5:22-23 says;
But the fruit of the Spirit is love, joy, peace, longsuffering, gentleness, goodness, faith, meekness, temperance: against such there is no law.

You will also see how the component of goodness comes into play in carrying out this instruction. Now, let's move on and get an understanding of the specificity of what the Holy Spirit was saying through Apostle Paul when He gave this verse.

We Beseech You

In 1 Thessalonians 5:12, the Greek word translated as beseech is *erōtáō* which literally means to 'beg' or 'pray' or 'urge.' Apostle Paul is literally begging christians to honour those that minister the Word to them and are over them in the Lord. This beseeching or begging is an intensifier of the issue on grieving the Holy Spirit. Apostle Paul had to beg and use this manner of speech because he recognized the gravity of what he was saying, and knew the consequences of disobeying this instruction.

I want you to see the contrast between the way he expresses himself in that passage versus the use of another Greek word that is also translated as 'beseech' in Apostle Peter's letter to the churches in 1 Peter:

1 Peter 2:11
Dearly beloved, I beseech you as strangers and pilgrims, abstain from fleshly lusts, which war against the soul.

Here the Greek word translated as 'beseech' is *parakaléō* which means to exhort or to urge. But when Paul talks about this subject we are touching on in the book of Thessalonians, he is literally pleading and begging—*erōtáō*—that christians know them that labour among them.

He could have chosen other words to employ here, but he intentionally chose *erōtáō* (begging) rather than *parakaléō* (only exhorting) as was used in 1 Peter 2:11. I know it may sound as if these things should be obvious to christians but walking in the spirit does not come naturally to those with a carnal mind and so Paul had to spell it out so they could understand. Anyway back to the book of Thessalonians, the other words that could have been used by the Apostle end at exhortation only but do not necessarily extend their meaning to include begging. Here in 1 Thessalonians 5:12, he shows the seriousness of this issue by exhorting and begging that the brethren would **"know them which labour among you, and are over you in the Lord, and admonish you; and esteem them very highly in love."**

I know most have never made the connection between what Paul was instructing here and the Holy Spirit. Consequently, they neglect their duties and responsibilities concerning those who are over them and minister things of the Spirit to them. As a result, they unwittingly hinder the work of the Spirit in their lives by quenching and stifling the Spirit.

What many fail to understand is that when you look at a man or woman of God, whatever spiritual gift they carry has been given by the Holy Spirit for the edification of the Church.

Ephesians 4:11-12
And He gave some, apostles; and some, prophets; and some, evangelists; and some, pastors and teachers; for the perfecting of the saints, for the work of the ministry, for the edifying of the Body of Christ.

That gift is not for the one who carries it. It is for the benefit of those that will receive the ministration of that minister. For example, the pastoral gift benefits the congregation of the pastor, not the man himself. When you fail to honour the one carrying such a gift, you actually hinder the working of the Holy Spirit in your life through that gift.

Now don't get me wrong on this one. I know there are some who might think that such honour is unnecessary, but it is imperative that Christians do not neglect those who are over them. In fact, this is precisely what Paul was talking about in his letter to the Philippians. Watch what the scripture says:

Philippians 4:16
For even in Thessalonica ye sent once and again unto my necessity. Not because I desire a gift: but I desire fruit that may abound to your account.

Paul is saying I am not accepting what you're giving just because I want to receive things from you, but that through the gift you are sending, there may be fruit or increase that comes to you. In other words, without that gift, the fruit or increase that should have come to the Philippian church by the power of the Spirit would not have come. There is a benefit that the Philippians were getting from the ministration of Paul, but they still lacked certain things until they started sending the gift that brought the increase and fruit to their account.

Right there, they would have short-circuited the power of God, poured water on the fire of the Spirit, and stopped their progress dead in its tracks. And on that wonderful afternoon when He came into my room, the Spirit of God began to show me through these scriptures and more how Christians frustrate the work of the Spirit in their lives. Paul begs the Thessalonians, as I do you today, to know them that are above you.

Frustrating the Grace of God

That message resonates throughout Paul's letters to the churches. It was no coincidence that this was the very first thing that the Holy Spirit began to teach me about. I cannot overemphasize this point because this is exactly how many of God's people are grieving the Spirit and frustrating the grace of God.

As you go through the scriptures, you can see Paul's *sunesis* or mindset concerning the issue. He is a man that was used by the Holy Spirit to write most of the New Testament and knew how to cooperate with the Holy Spirit. Watch what the scripture says in the book of Corinthians:

1 Corinthians 16:17-18
I am glad of the coming of Stephanas and Fortunatus and Achaicus: for that which was lacking on your part they have

supplied. For they have refreshed my spirit and yours: *therefore* [emphasis added] acknowledge ye them that are such.

Apostle Paul says men of God and workers of God should be acknowledged because they refresh our spirits. He was acknowledging Stephanas, Fortunatus, and Achaicus for supplying what the Christians lacked. Paul said, "they have refreshed my spirit and yours," meaning these men had something spiritual to give. They were used of the Holy Spirit to minister to the Corinthians. For that reason, the instruction immediately follows, "acknowledge ye them that are such."

Now when Paul says acknowledge them, he doesn't just mean when you meet them in the street greet them as such, oh no! The Greek word translated as 'acknowledge,' is *epiginōskō* which means to become fully acquainted with. In other words, know how they are taken care of and their well-being. Now I know some are thinking that the instruction only had to do with the people that Paul mentioned by name. I don't want you to miss this. He actually said it this way: "acknowledge ye them that are such," meaning that everybody that is used by God to refresh your spirit should be acknowledged in the same manner, not just the ones named in that passage of scripture. Paul was instructing them on what should be the norm when it comes to dealing with those who are above you in the Lord.

You need to understand that for your pastor to say to you, "Oh, just call me John, not Pastor John." might be his humility, but it would still be pride on your part to take that as the norm. When you address a pastor as such, you fail to acknowledge the office appointed to them by the Holy Spirit, and just by that, you grieve the Spirit of God.

Apostle Paul once made a comment that grieved the Holy Spirit.

Yes, I really mean Apostle Paul. He made a statement that the Holy Spirit did not find comforting. The Apostle Paul touched the Lord's anointed by scolding a man of God! When the high priest Ananias commanded them that stood by Paul to beat him up, notice how he responded:

Acts 23:2-3
And the high priest Ananias commanded them that stood by him to smite him on the mouth. Then said Paul unto him, God shall smite thee, thou whited wall: for sittest thou to judge me after the law, and commandest me to be smitten contrary to the law?

In all honesty, Apostle Paul was right: The Law allowed the high priest to judge but did not allow him to slap or beat him. However, his outburst was not allowed by the Holy Spirit. In his being right, he was gravely wrong. In his sincerity, he was sincerely wrong.

The Problem of Paul

To show you how easily even seasoned and mature christians can fall into this trap and grieve the Spirit of God, let's bear in mind that this is the same Apostle Paul who the Holy Spirit used to write fourteen books of the Bible. You see, Paul did not walk with the Lord during his earthly ministry as the other apostles had. He was a man that had been schooled by the Holy Spirit Himself and the one who gave us the instructions on how not to quench the Spirit.

Apostle Paul is the one who penned the scriptures that speak of not grieving the Holy Spirit. He is also the one who spoke of not resisting the Holy Spirit. However, when he said what he said in Acts 23:3, he had done the opposite of what the Holy Spirit wants.

Watch how the people responded to his outbursts:

Honouring Those Sent of God

Acts 23:4
And they that stood by said, "Revilest thou God's high priest?" Then said Paul, "I wist not, brethren, that he was the high priest: for it is written, Thou shalt not speak evil of the ruler of thy people."

Now I know this is where most people miss it right here. The apostle Paul is not apologising because what he had said was wrong, oh no! He had stated the facts. That man should not have struck him according to the Law. But the law that says that the high priest should not have struck him is superseded by the one that says, "thou shalt not speak evil of the ruler of thy people," which is why Apostle Paul immediately went to that scripture. Paul understood that even though he was more learned than the high Priest, he needed to submit to the designated authority of God and that takes humility and meekness, which is attribute of the fruit of the Spirit.

Many christians think that when a man of God falls short, it gives them a license to kill. If that is what you think, you are sadly mistaken. The gifts and callings of God are without repentance. That man is still as called by God as he was before he sinned or fell short of what you may think is good.

Paul is saying, despite the high priest's wrongdoing, because he is the ruler of our people, the Spirit of God does not permit me to speak against him. Brothers and sisters, you stop the work of the Holy Spirit in your own life when you lift your voice to speak against the Lord's anointed. You are grieving the Spirit of God and frustrating everything He is trying to accomplish in your life.

Pay close attention to how the Apostle responded. Sure, the high priest was wrong, but notice Paul's response to what the people said about him not being allowed by God to do what he did, even if the man of God that beat him up was wrong.

Acts 23:5
Then said Paul, "I wist not, brethren, that he was the high priest: for it is written, Thou shalt not speak evil of the ruler of thy people."

Apostle Paul immediately saw the consequences of his actions and quoted Exodus 22:28b **"Thou shalt not revile God, nor curse the ruler of thy people."**

Remember, this is Paul we are talking about. No doubt he was more anointed than this high priest. But when he spoke up against the man, he was not just touching the person; he also touched the One who put him in that office and what it represents. This is what most christians fail to realise. Because of their ignorance, they have written articles upon articles slandering men and women of God not knowing that it is to their own undoing.

"The ruler of thy people," as Apostle Paul declared, is the same as the Word proclaims where it says that the man of God that God has given you is a ruler over you. Watch what the scripture says in the book of Hebrews:

Hebrews 13:17
Obey them that have the rule over you, and submit yourselves: for they watch for your souls...

This is something the people of God have fail to see. They have written books and books and volumes more to revile men God has called and sent. They have written articles in the press and gossiped about the people that God has commanded that they should not curse. It is a shame that people do not see what the Lord wants from those who are really sanctified.

When Paul realised he had spoken against the high priest, he stopped immediately to acknowledge his wrong and changed his tone. The high priest was not even a christian or follower of Christ. He was a sinner in the stickiest sense. But because he held a position in the Jewish religious seat, he was an anointed man who could not be touched even by the lips of a man more anointed than him. Paul was not qualified to talk against him even though the high priest was not born again.

The world we are in is full of christians who gossip about men and women of God and could not care less what the consequences are. The christians of today are stiff-necked and do not "know" those that are above them.

Acts 7:51
Ye stiff-necked and uncircumcised in heart and ears, ye do always resist the Holy Ghost: as your fathers did, so do ye.

"Uncircumcised in heart[s] and ears" pointed out the fact that though his audience had been circumcised in the literal sense and thus bore upon their bodies the sign of the Abrahamic covenant, their hearts were untouched, unbroken, and unavailable to the voice of God as spoken by his Holy Spirit. They were resisting the Holy Spirit. This means that they were wilfully thwarting His leading by disobedience or rebellion.

Know Them

To "know," what the Apostle Paul wanted the christians to do, we should understand *knaris* the word that means to understand and recognise. This is a spiritual action that should be fed in the Spirit and come produce an action on the outside. It does not only mean to see a man and proclaim before all, "He is a man of God!" It means to recognise as in seeing to their need and also respecting them as vessels used by God to bring His message. Everyone is a vessel, but some have a particular role that they are chosen to fulfil, and it is to your advantage to honour them accordingly.

For instance, in Matthew it says:

Matthew 10:41
He that receives a prophet in the name of a prophet, shall receive a prophet's reward.

This lets us know that there is a distinction to the office of a prophet that when acknowledged brings you benefit. The bible tells us that every good and perfect gift comes from above meaning that there are certain good things that God cannot give until you learn to acknowledge the giftings and callings of the Spirit as such. That scripture is literally telling you that when you recognise and distinguish those that labour among you and minister spiritual things, it is something that God rewards. And when you fail to honour and acknowledge those who are above you, the opposite is also true. In other words, not only do you grieve the Holy Spirit of God, but you also forfeit your reward. There are certain things you are going without right now simply due to the mere fact that you fail to acknowledge or "know them which labour among you."

Watching for Their Need

Seeing to it that the needs of the man or woman God put in your life are met is not a very popular subject among professing christians. This ought not to stop the truth from being put forward. Apostle Paul grappled with this very issue and went to great lengths to defend his position on the matter. Watch what the scripture says:

1 Corinthians 9:11
If we have sown into your life spiritual things, is it too much if we get carnal [material] things from you?"

Apostle Paul here is elucidating the fact that no amount of money or value of things is great enough to be given in exchange for the Word of God. Spiritual things are priceless. Nonetheless, he is making the point that those who minister spiritual things ought to be honoured with the substance of those who are receiving the ministration. In fact, what Paul is saying is that they are within their rights to make that demand. To deny them this right would grieve the Holy Spirit.

Now I must point out to you here that there is no way you will be able to follow that instruction unless that attribute of the fruit of the Spirit which is called goodness is at work in you.

Galatians 5:22-23
But the fruit of the Spirit is love, joy, peace, longsuffering, gentleness, goodness, faith, meekness, temperance: against such there is no law.

The Greek word translated as goodness in that passage is agathosyne, which means uprightness of heart and kindness. Paul is actually emphasising what the fruit of the Spirit should produce in you. You want to know whether or not you have the fruit of the Spirit just watch how you honour those above. It will point you to what is inside of you, the real ugly truth. Anyway, I will live that unpopular one alone for now, let's move on.

Ministers Who Frustrate the Grace

On the other hand, I must also point out that there is a danger that if ignored will also cause the quenching of the Spirit. That danger lies in ministers of the Gospel abusing this privilege and grieving the Spirit of God as a result. You need to understand that all things work by love in the Kingdom of God. And as much as a minister of the Gospel is entitled to certain provisions, greed will

Hello Holy Spirit

lead to some making unreasonable demands and abusing their positions. Nevertheless, this does not mean that we can neglect our responsibilities when it comes to supporting those who minister the Gospel.

Many do not understand what real ministers go through, yet they simply want to be them. They want to walk on the water, but are they ready to face the dangers of almost falling or sinking because of the wind? People want what they see the man of God doing from the pulpit, but they are completely ignorant of what that same man of God goes through at night when no one else is around. The man of God is expected to deliver every time all the time, but few are willing to honour that.

Some say that pastors should not receive any compensation at all, and to that they should follow the admonition of Jesus who said:

Matthew 10:8
Freely you received, freely give.

Others argue that pastors who are truly spiritual should decline being paid. These two arguments might sound good, but are they valid? Let's take a look.

First, let's examine the context of Jesus' words in Matthew 10:8:

Matthew 10:5-11
5 These twelve Jesus sent out after instructing them: "Do not go in the way of the Gentiles, and do not enter any city of the Samaritans; 6 but rather go to the lost sheep of the house of Israel. 7 And as you go, preach, saying, 'The kingdom of heaven is at hand. 8 Heal the sick, raise the dead, cleanse the lepers, cast out demons. Freely you received, freely give. 9 Do not acquire gold, or silver, or copper for your money belts, 10 or a bag for your journey, or even two coats, or sandals, or a staff; for the

worker is worthy of his support. 11 And whatever city or village you enter, inquire who is worthy in it, and stay at his house until you leave that city."

Now, the biggest problem here is that we have too many people that just hang on to one particular side of the scripture without even looking at the context of the passage. This leads to wrong doctrine. The context of this statement is dealing with healing the sick, raising the dead, cleansing the lepers, and casting out demons. What is interesting is that in the next two verses Jesus said take along no money (gold or silver), then he says in verse 10, "for the worker is worthy of his support." The implication is that those who are preaching the Gospel and performing the ministry that Christ has given them should be supported by those people to whom they minister. Also, by looking at similar verses we find the same message.

Another key scripture I want you to see is found in the first few verses of Luke 9:

Luke 9:1-5
And He called the twelve together, and gave them power and authority over all the demons and to heal diseases. 2 And He sent them out to proclaim the kingdom of God and to perform healing. 3 And He said to them, "Take nothing for your journey, neither a staff, nor a bag, nor bread, nor money; and do not even have two tunics apiece. 4 Whatever house you enter, stay there until you leave that city. 5 And as for those who do not receive you, as you go out from that city, shake the dust off your feet as a testimony against them."

Clearly Jesus told the disciples to accept the support offered them in their ministry; that is, they were to enter a house and stay there. If they were not being formally paid, then they must be housed and fed. Should we conclude that ministers of the Word should stay with the people they preach to and be dependent on them? Not at all! In fact, we even find that when Jesus was carrying out His earthly ministry, He and His disciples had a money box (which, unfortunately, Judas would steal from).

Jesus was telling the disciples to trust God as they ministered. That is why He said, "Do not acquire gold, or silver, or copper for your money belt" (Matthew 10:9). But an interesting change of teaching by Jesus can be found in Luke when later on in His ministry He told the disciples to take a purse, a bag, and a sword.

Luke 22:35-38
And He said to them, "When I sent you out without money belt and bag and sandals, you did not lack anything, did you?" They said, "No, nothing." 36 And He said to them, "But now, whoever has a money belt is to take it along, likewise also a bag, and whoever has no sword is to sell his coat and buy one. 37 For I tell you that this which is written must be fulfilled in Me, 'And He was numbered with transgressors;' for that which refers to Me has its fulfillment." 38 They said, "Lord, look, here are two swords." And He said to them, "It is enough."

Why the change? It was because soon the disciples would be without Jesus and they would have to rely on God's provision through people, not through Christ, during their upcoming Gospel work.

What Does Paul Say?

Some people think because Paul worked as a tentmaker as he travelled around that he was against people being paid for what they do in ministry. Apostle Paul has several things to say about following Christ and money. Let's take a closer look at Apostle Paul's dealings.

2 Thessalonians 3:9-10
Not because we have not power, but to make ourselves an ensample unto you to follow us. For even when we were with you, this we commanded you, that if any would not work, neither should he eat.

Now, in that particular passage, Apostle Paul is dealing with disorderly conduct. He specifically addressing those who were meddling in other people's affairs and refusing to work. That is why he gives a command that those who refuse to work shouldn't eat. Even though he encourages us to follow his example of working, he was a staunch advocate for the support of those in ministry, himself included. Let's look in further detail at what he said to the church at Corinth:

1 Corinthians 9:1-6
1 Am I not free? Am I not an apostle? Have I not seen Jesus our Lord? Are you not my work in the Lord? 2 If to others I am not an apostle, at least I am to you; for you are the seal of my apostleship in the Lord. 3 My defence to those who examine me is this: 4 Do we not have a right to eat and drink? 5 Do we not have a right to take along a believing wife, even as the rest of the apostles and the brothers of the Lord and Cephas? 6 Or do only Barnabas and I not have a right to refrain from working? 7 Who at any time serves as a soldier at his own expense? Who plants a vineyard and does not eat the fruit of it? Or who tends a flock and does not use the milk of the flock?

Paul obviously felt he was in part rejected and his credentials as an apostle were doubted. He was an apostle like Peter (Cephas) and the other apostles, yet he was not honoured in the same way. Paul felt his brothers in Christ were held in a celebrity status position. Consequently, people were biased and paid more attention to them while ignoring him and Barnabas. The level of

Paul's anointing was high, but he realized the people were more hung up on popularity rather than the anointing. Because of that, they were giving to others more than he and Barnabas were receiving as apostles.

The other apostles, with the exception of Paul and Barnabas, were paid and did not have to work. Apostle Paul complained bitterly about it and was accused as being "cheap." In response, Paul defends his right to be remunerated as the other apostles were. His strong arguments and irrefutable analogies validated his right to be supported and rewarded for his labour.

Apostle Paul was not merely voicing his personal opinion. He provides scriptural evidence from the Law in support of his position:

1 Corinthians 9:8-10
8 Do I say these things as a mere man? Or does not the law say the same also? 9 For it is written in the law of Moses, 'You shall not muzzle an ox while it treads out the grain.' Is it oxen God is concerned about? 10 Or does He say it altogether for our sakes? For our sakes, no doubt, this is written, that he who plows should plow in hope, and he who threshes in hope should be partaker of his hope.

In the Old Testament days, it was against the law to muzzle the oxen that walked on the grain to thresh out the sheaves. The oxen were working, so they deserved to eat. That was a requirement in Israel. If oxen had the right to receive from the fruit of their labour, how much more the man of God who ministers day and night. To drive his point home, Paul asks, "Was God thinking only about oxen when He said this?" Then he answers, "No! This was written for our sakes." To paraphrase Martin Luther, "oxen can't read. It was written for us, not the oxen."

I might add, parenthetically, that is a very important principle to remember when reading the Old Testament. All those regulations that were given to Israel concerning their diet, their work, their clothing, etc., were not given to them only, they were given for us. They are pictures of what God is teaching us. If you read the Old Testament with that in mind, you will have a whole new book before you.

Just in case there is any lingering doubt about Apostle Paul's position on whether those who labour in the Gospel should be paid, let's look at the next few verses:

1 Corinthians 9:11-14
11 If we have sown spiritual things for you, is it a great thing if we reap your material things? 12 If others share the right over you, do we not more? Nevertheless, we did not use this right, but we endure all things so that we will cause no hindrance to the Gospel of Christ. 13 Do you not know that those who perform sacred services eat the food of the temple, and those who attend regularly to the altar have their share from the altar? 14 So also the Lord directed those who proclaim the Gospel to get their living from the Gospel.

The people really didn't "know" or recognise Paul and Barnabas as those that were over them in the Lord. Apostle Paul was indignant about this lack of understanding. Paul was operating at a high level with regards to the anointing, even higher than the other apostles, and should have been honoured as such. With the declaration "Those who proclaim the Gospel get their living from the Gospel." Paul states his unqualified right to be paid for faithfully proclaiming the Gospel. He acknowledges that he did not exercise his right because he felt he might somehow hinder the Gospel, but the right itself was no longer up for debate.

Worthy of Double Honour

When Papa Hagin was starting out in the ministry, he would travel to various places across the country preaching the Gospel. As he visited different churches and ministered, sometimes the most he would get when he was finished was a handshake. The times he would be given an honorarium, it might not even be large enough to put petrol in his car for his return home. He was lightly esteemed and not given his due honour.

What Papa Hagin experienced might have been due to the character of the Pastor or the level he thought brother Hagin was moving in. they failed to recognise those that are above them and to give honour where it is due. Had it been another preacher of great renown maybe he would have treated him differently. You need to understand that Papa Hagin at that time was just coming up. He was not the Papa Hagin we know now. It might then have been an issue of the pastor thinking this is just an ordinary preacher; I'll do what I need to do but only to a certain extent. Am I saying that is right? No way! That's the evil the Holy Spirit helped me to see. In America, a preacher from Africa can be remunerated using peanuts, yet he or she will be hearing God. But what drives most of America's popular Christian world is the issue of celebrity preachers. They are treated better and honoured more than some unknown preachers who are truly anointed. But these things ought not to be so.

Apostle Paul further elucidates on this issue in his instructions to young Timothy concerning elders:

1 Timothy 5:17-18 RSV
Let the elders who rule well be considered worthy of double honor, especially those who labour in preaching and teaching; 18 for the scripture says, "You shall not muzzle an ox when it is treading out the grain," and, "The labourer deserves his wages."

Honouring Those Sent of God

Paul is clearly referring to those who he called bishops in chapter 3 of this letter to Timothy. The word 'bishops' there means overseers or those in oversight. That is also what the elders were. The word 'elder' refers to the man—his maturity, his experience, etc. The words 'bishop' or 'overseer' refer to his work. An elder is responsible for overseeing a congregation, to be aware of what is happening and be concerned about it.

It is unfortunate that the word 'rule' is used here about an elder's work: "Let the elders who rule well..." That word implies that these men are bosses, that they are somehow in charge or lords or governors in a congregation. But actually, the word is better translated 'leads.' So, the verse could be read, "Let the elders who lead well be worthy of double honour."

A leader does not boss people around; he leads them, going before and setting the pace and the direction. Whether people follow or not depends entirely upon how much respect he has built in their eyes by his personal character, his abilities, and his gifts. An elder is a man who is able to command the respect of others and get them to follow him in the directions the Lord has set.

Because Paul refers to elders who "labour in preaching and teaching," some people believe there are two classes of elders: ruling elders and teaching elders. But there is really only one class. All elders are to preach and teach. In fact, in verse 2 of chapter 3, one of the listed qualifications for an elder is that he be "apt to teach." That is how he leads a congregation. Unless an elder is preaching or teaching from the scriptures, he is not leading for the scriptures set the direction of life. That is what constitutes the work of an elder.

The statement "those who rule well" implies that not all rule well. There are those who do not "labour in the word and doctrine," so a distinction is being made. As was said, all elders are to preach and to teach, but some labour in this. Some devote long hours to extensive preparation; they teach often and scarcely have enough time left to earn a living in other ways. The apostle says that those who "labour in preaching and teaching" and have the skills, gifts and abilities to do so, are to be given "double honour." Respect is to be given to all elders and pastors. That is the first honour. Remuneration is the second.

The subject of remuneration in the Church is for some an extremely sensitive one. People often balk at the notion of paying preachers and teachers. I personally have never received a salary from my church organisation because I have businesses that the Lord helped me and my wife BeBe to start which are very successful so we don't need to be paid because we have the money to take care of ourselves. In fact, we sponsor the organisation from our own pockets most times. That being said, it doesn't mean preachers are to be like us. They need to be taken care of because here the scripture is clear: those who labour in the Word and doctrine should be paid. Those who would be diligent in the Word and in prayer need the time and the means to make that possible.

Acts 6:2, 5
Then the twelve called the multitude of the disciples unto them, and said, It is not reason that we should leave the word of God, and serve tables. But we will give ourselves continually to prayer, and to the ministry of the word.

The leaders of the early Church recognized the importance of undistracted devotion to the things of God. Their primary responsibility in the Church was to oversee the care of God's people, bringing them up in the nurture and admonition of the Word. It is as necessary now as it was in the early Church. Therefore, the needs, expenses, and salaries of those who

Honouring Those Sent of God

faithfully discharge their duties in teaching and preaching the Word of God should be maintained on their behalf. This enables them to be free to do the work of preaching and teaching instead of concentrating on other jobs. Otherwise, they are limited in their capacity to fully work for God and His people. The conclusive basis for pastors' salaries is this: if they are fully occupied in this work of preaching and teaching the Scriptures so that people understand them, then they are to be given double honour.

The principle Paul is highlighting is that those who labour deserve their wages. In fact, he quotes these words of Jesus, "The labourer deserves his wages" (Luke 10:7 RSV). That is intriguing because that could mean the Gospel of Luke was already in existence when Paul quoted the Lord's words from it. Another possibility is this was a word spoken by the Lord that was widely circulated orally at that time. Either way, Paul refers to it as the Lord's own confirmation of this principle.

Deserving of Goodness

Let us go back for a moment to the scripture "freely you have received, freely give" (Matthew 10:8) and look at it in the light of another very important scripture:

Galatians 6:6
Let him that is taught in the Word communicate unto him that teacheth in all good things.

Two specific categories of people are being referred to here: the ones teaching, and the ones being taught. To put it another way, one is giving, and one is receiving. Do you see that? When we look at the verse which says, "freely you have received, freely give," many christians have developed a one-sided mentality in thinking that the teacher is the one who received (the Word), so he or she should be the one to freely give (the Word), but that is a misconception. The Gospel may be distributed freely, but it is not free. It costs somebody something.

There are those who labour in the Word. They spend time in prayer seeking revelation. They search the Scriptures and study the Word to dig out hidden treasures that can then be given to you. While you are sleeping, they are seeking the face of God, not for themselves, but for you. They spend time ministering to you, sometimes away from their spouses and children, just so they can bring the Word of the Lord to you. Which part of any of that would you consider "freely received?"

It is not the one who has laboured in the Word who has freely received. It is you, the recipient, the one who freely receives the Word which comes to you as the fruit or result of another one's labour. Therefore, since you are the one who has freely received, it behoves you to follow the next instruction, "freely give."

Let's look again at the scripture in Galatians 6:6:

Let him that is taught in the Word communicate unto him that teacheth in all good things.

That word 'communicate,' also rendered 'share' in other translations, is the Greek word *koinōnéō*. This word should have a ring of familiarity because it is very close to the word *koinōnía* which I have talked about in the previous chapter. *Koinōnéō* means 'to share, contribute, distribute,' and each of these involves you personally. So, it's not just 'share, contribute, distribute,' it's 'I share,' 'I contribute,' 'I distribute.' That means, if you are the one who is being "taught in the Word," you are the one who should share, contribute, distribute to the person who has been teaching you. And in case you're wondering what you should share, contribute, or distribute, it's right there in the text: "all good things." This is not referring to a simple pat on the back and a "Good job!" It says, "things."

A good thing is whatever is for the recipient's convenience and advantage. As a matter of fact, that verse is specifically referring to external goods and riches. So, if we were to paraphrase Galatians 6:6 using a more literal translation based on what we now understand, it might look something like this:

Let the person who is being taught in the Word share, contribute, distribute all kinds of external goods and riches for the convenience and advantage of the one who has laboured in the Word to teach them.

That should put an end to the question of whether a man or woman of God should receive a salary or any other "good thing" for that matter.

It cannot be coincidental that this instruction is in the chapter that immediately follows the chapter which speaks of the fruit of the Spirit. You see, giving in the spirit of love is never done under compulsion. Love gives freely. Love is manifested and demonstrated in goodness, *agathósuné*, which is also translated 'generosity.' When you walk in the Spirit, you walk in love which manifests itself in generosity. Goodness is more than mere disposition. It encompasses that, but it is more than that. It is an action of beneficence, goodness which is acted out in generosity and charitable deeds towards others. If you are walking in love, you will not fail to honour in the form of giving "good things" to the man or woman of God who has sown spiritual things into your life.

On the other hand, if a pastor or an elder is not teaching and feeding the flock, then it is wrong to support him. Mind you, I did not say it is wrong to respect him. But if he is not carrying out the duties of his office, let him work for a living like everyone else. If, however, he is teaching and feeding the flock, make it possible for him to have the time and means to do so. That is the idea. We pay pastors because we set them aside for this work. But those who preach and teach (which all elders are supposed to do) and also earn a living otherwise, we call elders. We distinguish between pastors and elders in that sense. If you understand that all elders are pastors, then you will get at the heart of what the passage in 1 Timothy 5:17-18 is saying.

Honour and Discipline

Discipline in the Church is one that ought to be handled with honour, particularly when it comes to the delicate matter of disciplining elders when they misbehave. This is a concern that Paul also addresses.

1 Timothy 5:19-20 RSV
Never admit any charge against an elder except on the evidence of two or three witnesses. As for those who persist in sin, rebuke them in the presence of all, so that the rest may stand in fear.

Bringing a charge against an elder is a serious matter not to be taken lightly. Whether he is fulfilling his duties or not, he is to be shown respect at all times. By the very nature of the office, elders and pastors are subject to public scrutiny. And if they have to say unpleasant things to people, as the case often requires, sometimes people strike back and try to get even. They may even slander the elder or start rumours. To minimize this, no charge against an elder should be entertained unless it is supported by more than one person.

I heard of a young pastor who had been dismissed suddenly by his board of elders. Charges had been levelled against him by a member of the congregation that proved unfounded. Unfortunately, the board believed it. It later came out that it was the pastor's personal secretary who had accused him. She was angry with the pastor, so she typed a letter containing very serious charges against him. She then presented the letter to the elders as though it were received from someone else. Without any further confirmation, the board relieved the young man of his responsibilities. The secretary eventually confessed her deceit, but the crushing blow had already been dealt with shattering implications to the pastor. Thankfully, God gave him the grace to overcome, but it is precisely such scenarios this verse is designed to eliminate.

That young pastor's painful experience serves as an example of why we should not entertain a charge against an elder unless it is supported by two or three witnesses. However, it does beg the question of what to do when the charges against an elder are indeed proven. The scriptures also provide practical guidance in this. The Lord Jesus said:

Matthew 18:15-17a NASB
15 If your brother sins, go and show him his fault in private; if he listens to you, you have won your brother. 16 But if he does not listen to you, take one or two more with you, so that by the mouth of two or three witnesses every fact may be confirmed. 17 If he refuses to listen to them, tell it to the church.

When a charge is confirmed and the elder repents, no public action is necessary. Nothing more needs to be said. That settles it. But if he persists, then a public rebuke is required:

1 Timothy 5:20 NASB
Those who continue in sin, rebuke in the presence of all, so that the rest also will be fearful of sinning.

A public rebuke is challenging but fundamental which is why Paul urges Timothy to do this in spite of how difficult it may be. A church that does not resolve to do that when it is required will lose its witness and diminish its effectiveness.

Many of you can relate to Timothy's position. He was not an elder or a pastor. Yet he was responsible, as we are, to call to the attention of leaders anything that is not in line with the scriptures. As concerned members of the Body of Christ, we must press for action in line with the Word. That is why the Scriptures were given to teach and correct us.

Points to Bear in Mind

Apostle Paul must have realized how difficult the undertaking of discipline in the church would be for young Timothy. With that in mind, he provides four key admonitions to bear in mind if anyone attempts to correct a congregation or stir the leadership to action. First, no partiality must be shown. Paul says:

1 Timothy 5:21 RSV
In the presence of God and of Christ Jesus and of the elect angels I charge you to keep these rules without favour, doing nothing from partiality.

Elders can be very strong-minded men. I know that for a fact. Timothy might well have felt intimidated by certain forceful personalities among the elderships and been afraid to take them on. That can happen. It would have been easy for Timothy to have shown partiality in such instances. He might very well have had some close friends among the leaders of the church at Ephesus. He very likely did since he was working with these men and was a lonely young man. But he could not afford to let any of that get in the way of doing what was necessary if an elder got out of line.

Timothy might have felt inadequate, but the apostle reminds him of his supernatural reinforcement: **"the presence of God and of Christ Jesus and of the elect angels."** God the Father is involved. He knows everything that is going on in a congregation, and nothing is hidden from His eyes. Christ Jesus as the Lord of the Church and the Head of the Body is present also and can work from within. He can touch men's consciences; He can reach their hearts. And the elect angels are involved, these glorious beings whom the book of Hebrews tells us are as:

Hebrews 1:14
Ministering spirits, sent forth to minister for them who shall be heirs of salvation.

Paul encourages Timothy not to be intimidated. If a situation requires action, do it patiently, lovingly, thoughtfully and carefully. But by all means, act.

Then Paul gives Timothy a second admonition: choose men carefully. A man said of a certain elder, "He's a good man, and he's almost honest." That does not qualify a man as an elder. An elder ought to be an honest man, not almost so. Sometimes men are put into office without any special care being exercised. The apostle cautions Timothy be very careful so that this won't happen. He says:

1 Timothy 5:22 RSV
Do not be hasty in the laying on of hands, nor participate in another man's sins; keep yourself pure.

Now, to appreciate the seriousness of what is being communicated here, we need to clarify the significance of "the laying on of hands." The laying on of hands represents the recognition of a man as being chosen by the Lord. It is a sign of approval and identification with that person. It does not confer anything. Rather, it signifies that such a man is one whom God has chosen. That distinction is crucial because it automatically places that person in a position of influence in the church. When that happens, everyone in the church is exposed to that person's influence, good or bad. Therefore, the character of the person should be examined over time. Otherwise, if someone is approved too quickly, it could have a detrimental impact especially if that one leads others to partake in his sinful lifestyle. That is why it is vitally important to take Paul's admonition seriously.

The next admonition the apostle gives might seem a rather strange one:

1 Timothy 5:23 RSV
No longer drink only water, but use a little wine for the sake of your stomach and your frequent ailments.

Was Paul recommending wine drinking for Christians? That is the question many people have when they read this verse. For some, the prospect of being able to drink alcohol gets them excited. Others get up in arms and are ready to dispatch the wine and alcohol police. But once the context is understood, you will see that it is much less complicated than some make it out to be.

There have been some very tortured and even humorous exegeses of this passage. I heard of a young man who sought to expound this verse. He was reading from the King James Version which says: "Drink no longer water, but use a little wine for thy stomach's sake." This preacher's incredible explanation was there were two kinds of liquid referred to here: there was wine (which was really grape juice), and there was what he called "longer water," which was liquor. According to him, the apostle's admonition is, stop drinking that longer water ("drink no longer water") but use a little wine for your stomach's sake. That is the kind of trouble you can get into when you work solely with the English text. A little knowledge is a dangerous thing!

We all know we need to drink water to survive. Common sense would tell us that when the apostle said "drink no longer water" he could not have been suggesting that we stop drinking water altogether. After all, Apostle Paul wasn't trying to kill us! The verse is more accurately rendered: "stop drinking water only," The key word being "only."

Paul here is not warning Timothy about the use of alcohol. He is warning him about the water! If you have travelled abroad in some countries where water is not potable, you know what Timothy was going through. He was suffering from Montezuma's revenge; he was doing the Mexican two-step. To put it plainly, the man had stomach issues, the kind that makes you very familiar with the lavatory. Paul is simply advising him to use a little wine to prevent that.

Timothy was one who would have welcomed Apostle Paul's admonition in the previous verse to "keep thyself pure." He was a dedicated young man who would surely have set aside anything in his personal life that might harm his ministry. But evidently, Timothy was leaning too far toward total abstinence from wine ignoring its medicinal value, and it was adversely affecting his health. Paul wanted Timothy to adopt a more balanced position. He says in effect, for your health's sake, don't do this.

The last point the apostle makes is that Timothy ought to observe men over a period of time:

1 Timothy 5:24-25 RSV
The sins of some men are conspicuous, pointing to judgment, but the sins of others appear later. So also good deeds are conspicuous; and even when they are not, they cannot remain hidden.

That is a wise word and in line with what the apostle has already said about not laying hands suddenly on any man. Paul knew God

Hello Holy Spirit

was at work in the congregation in Ephesus, and He was revealing things that were being done behind closed doors. Jesus said, a time is coming when that which is done in secret will be shouted from the housetops, and that which is spoken in the closet will be broadcast in the streets (Luke 12:3). Everybody will know about it. People fool themselves into thinking that they can hide their sins, but God knows how to take hidden sins and bring them out into the light.

Some men's sins are conspicuous enough that it is obvious they are heading for God's judgment. You would not elect them or appoint them to any office. But the apostle warns that there is a more dangerous kind who are skilful at hiding their sin. They appear to be very dedicated, committed people, but there is evil lurking in their hearts the whole time. If you get into the habit of electing people to office or appointing them to some responsible position without giving time to observe them, you will get into trouble. As the saying goes, "Time has a big mouth. If you give anything enough time, it will tell you everything you need to know." Let some time go by and give God the opportunity to expose what needs to be exposed. Observe men closely and their deeds, whether good or evil, will become obvious.

All these things we are going through will simply direct you into how to have fruit of the Spirit in your live which is love, brothers and sisters that is how you walk in the spirit, when you walk in love. The things that the Holy Spirit began to teach me on that day will transform your life if you will only open up your heart to receive and as we get into this fifth chapter I need you to follow very carefully as we go deeper into the things of the spirit.

CHAPTER FIVE

Warn Them That Are Unruly

One of the most important things that the Holy Spirit began to teach me from the passage of scripture in 1 Thessalonians 5 is about those that are unruly.

1 Thessalonians 5:14
Now we exhort you, brethren, warn them that are unruly...

There are two key requirements of the fruit of the Spirit connected to this verse. One must be walked out by the one who warns; the other by the one being warned. Apostle Paul employs the Greek word *nouthetéō* which is translated "warn." That word, as it is used there, does not have a strictly harsh connotation as it might seem at first glance though chastisement can be involved. It means to reason with someone by cautioning or reproving them with gentleness. So, the component of love is required to warn the unruly is gentleness. You there are some people out there who just derive the greatest pleasure from pointing out somebody else's wrongs. They are so quick to say, "look now what is happening, I told you so".

This is not what the Paul is talking about, here, this reproving out of love and concern for the well-being of the one concerned. The unruly must then respond to that warning with the component of the fruit of Spirit called self-control. To understand why this is so, we first need to know who the unruly are.

Now, when we see that word 'unruly,' I know some of you immediately think of Sister So-and-so who is always making noise and being disruptive in church. But that is not who Apostle Paul is talking about. The unruly being referred to here are those who break rank. The Greek word translated as 'unruly' in that passage is *átaktos*, and it literally means insubordinate. We serve a God of order, and when people rebel and refuse to follow the order of God, they grieve the Spirit of God.

We would be seeing greater miracles in the Church today if people would only learn that God is a God of order. When you begin to break rank and go against your leadership, you frustrate the grace of God and grieve His Holy Spirit.

A typical example in scripture is that of Aaron and Miriam. They decided to challenge the authority of Moses when he took for himself an Ethiopian wife against the commandment of God. Watch what the scripture says:

Numbers 12:1-2
And Miriam and Aaron spake against Moses because of the Ethiopian woman whom he had married: for he had married an Ethiopian woman. And they said, hath the Lord indeed spoken only by Moses? Hath he not spoken also by us? And the Lord heard it.

Now you would have thought that Aaron and Miriam were due some sort of reward. After all, they were speaking up against this man of God who had broken the Law. They were not mistaken at all because by taking an Ethiopian bride, the man of God was violating the same law he had delivered to them himself.
If it had been in this day and age, he would have made the cover of *Time* magazine as a scandalous preacher. And all the Christian bloggers would be online tweeting about the juicy details. Let's see how the Lord responded in scripture:

Numbers 12:5
And the Lord came down in the pillar of the cloud, and stood in the door of the tabernacle, and called Aaron and Miriam: and they both came forth.

When the Lord called Aaron and Miriam forth, they must have stepped out shoulders square and heads held high. After all, they had defended the commandment of God against one dodgy prophet. But watch what the Lord had to say on the matter:

Numbers 12:6-11
6 And He said, "Hear now My words: if there be a prophet among you, I the Lord will make myself known unto him in a vision, and will speak unto him in a dream. 7 My servant Moses is not so, who is faithful in all mine house. 8 With him will I speak mouth to mouth, even apparently, and not in dark speeches; and the similitude of the Lord shall he behold: wherefore then were ye not afraid to speak against my servant Moses?" 9 And the anger of the Lord was kindled against them; and He departed. 10 And the cloud departed from off the tabernacle; and, behold, Miriam became leprous, white as snow: and Aaron looked upon Miriam, and, behold, she was leprous. 11 And Aaron said unto Moses, "Alas, my lord, I beseech thee, lay not the sin upon us, wherein we have done foolishly, and wherein we have sinned."

To their surprise, the Lord was furious; not with Moses who had broken the law, but with them for standing up against him. You see, the biggest epidemic in Christianity today is that we think we have been called to correct and police those who have been put in authority by God. And by doing so, we break rank and grieve the Spirit of God through our words and actions. Such a one becomes *átaktos*, unruly. You want to know how to walk in the spirit? Don't break rank!

Hello Holy Spirit

Aaron and Miriam had also broken the law, and their offence far outweighed that which they were accusing Moses of breaking. Remember the devil himself was booted out of Heaven because of the sin of rebellion. He broke rank and wanted to mount his throne above the Most High. Being unruly, *átaktos*, is the most devilish thing a christian is capable of doing. When you rebel against your spiritual authority, you are not just rebelling against the man you are gossiping about; you are rebelling against the God who gave him that authority and that grieves the Spirit of God.

It is evil when you are in a choir and gossip about the choir leader behind his or her back. It is amazing that this is such a common occurrence in the Church today!

As the Spirit of the Lord continued to minister to me that day, it became crystal clear how some of the things we don't even stop to think about hinder our spiritual progress. It is simply because we keep grieving the Holy Spirit. A man of God can stand in front and instruct the congregation to raise their hands to the Lord, and you will always find a few bozos that feel they are an exception to the instruction. You forget that the man that is telling you to raise your hands has been called and anointed to give you direction in that ministration. You may not have felt the urge to raise your hands. But if God is speaking to him, that this is what the congregation needs to do, then you are disobeying God Himself and breaking rank. Can you imagine what would have become of the prophet Samuel if he had not learnt how to listen and obey those appointed by God to be spiritual authorities? He would have negated his destiny altogether. I know some are confused now. Let me explain.

The very first time God spoke to Samuel as a prophet, the voice that Samuel heard was that of Eli the priest. Eli was the man to whom Samuel was brought when his mother fulfilled her vow to the Lord. Samuel was mentored by Eli from a tender age, and even though Eli was not a prophet, young Samuel understood the authority he had. Let's look at it from the scriptures:

1 Samuel 3:1-7
1 And the child Samuel ministered unto the Lord before Eli... 2 And it came to pass at that time, when Eli was laid down in his place, and his eyes began to wax dim, that he could not see; 3 And ere the lamp of God went out in the temple of the Lord, where the ark of God was, and Samuel was laid down to sleep; 4 That the Lord called Samuel: and he answered, Here am I. 5 And he ran unto Eli, and said, Here am I; for thou calledst me. And he said, I called not; lie down again. And he went and lay down. 6 And the Lord called yet again, Samuel. And Samuel arose and went to Eli, and said, Here am I; for thou didst call me. And he answered, I called not, my son; lie down again. 7 Now Samuel did not yet know the Lord, neither was the word of the Lord yet revealed unto him.

Now notice here that the scripture says that Samuel did not know the Lord neither did He have any revelation of the Word. So, the only way God could speak to him is if he understood spiritual authority. God was speaking, and Samuel kept going back to Eli and God never stopped him. How many things have you missed by failing to listen to the spiritual authority that God has placed over your life? Some have quenched the Spirit of God and completely missed their destiny simply because they fail to recognise those that God has put in authority over their lives.

When God first spoke to Samuel, it was in the middle of the night; Samuel was sleeping when he heard the voice of old Eli calling him. If it were some of you reading this passage right now, you would have just thought, *here we go again, another chore! Just when I'm about to fall asleep, he wants me to take out the trash! Let me just pretend I didn't hear*. (Now I didn't mention your name, so please keep reading. Nobody knows.) But not Samuel. Each time he got right up until Eli directed him to the source of the voice.

Imagine, God did not use the voice of his mother Hannah who loved him so much. Instead, it was the voice of one who was his spiritual authority that God chose to use. Samuel could have quenched the Spirit of God right then and there, but thank God he knew how to listen to authority. He could have broken rank and chosen to ignore that voice, but that ability to follow authority ensured he did not miss God that night.

What would happen if a general in the army gave an order and his commanding officer chose to completely ignore it just because he didn't get the memo? That officer would be court-martialled and reprimanded to the fullest extent of the law for sure. Yet in the kingdom of God, christians are failing to master this simple thing that even the carnal world has mastered.

Even demons don't break rank. Watch what the scripture says:

Mark 3:23-24
And He called them unto Him, and said unto them in parables, "How can Satan cast out Satan? And if a kingdom be divided against itself, that kingdom cannot stand."

Remember, the Lord was answering the scribes who had accused Him of casting out devils using Beelzebub prince of demons. Demons know not to break rank, but we have christians that do it without even giving it a second thought. That Greek word translated as 'cast out' is *ekballó*, and it doesn't only mean to drive out, but it also means to deprive of power and influence. That is exactly what happens when you break rank, you undermine the authority of the ones who God has placed over you and by so doing the ministration of the Spirit of God through those gifts in your own life.

Remember what the scripture says in the book of Romans:

Romans 13:1
Let every soul be subject unto the higher powers. For there is no power but of God: the powers that be are ordained of God.

Not being subject to the higher powers is like beating up a police officer because you caught him littering the park where your kids play, then asking that no charges be filed against you. The crime that you have just committed by beating up an officer of the law far outweighs the one he committed by littering. What makes assaulting an officer of the law an even more egregious offence is that by doing so, you defy the authority of the government he represents.

The Lord said to Aaron and Miriam, you know I speak to Moses face to face. In other words, I have separated him, and you should have recognised that in speaking against him you are speaking against My authority. Many people think that as long as they think what they are saying is accurate, then it's okay to speak against the authority of God. You are wrong. You have just become unruly, and you are grieving the Spirit of God. It's your duty to pray for those in authority rather than gossip about what you think is wrong.

God is more than capable of correcting and judging his delegated authority without your help. I always like to use this example. It's like when the CEO of a company makes a mistake, then you try to bankrupt the whole organisation for the mistake of that one man. The only problem with that is the CEO is also just an employee of that organisation, and the major shareholder, who is the real owner of the business, will fight tooth and nail to keep his business afloat.

That is exactly what happens when you start fighting a man of God. Because he is delegated authority, the one who actually responds is the Owner of the work that you are now trying to pull down. That is why Gamaliel, who was a doctor of the Law, warned the Pharisees against persecuting the disciples for preaching in the name of Jesus. Watch what the scripture says:

Acts 5: 38-39
And now I say unto you, refrain from these men, and let them alone: for if this counsel or this work be of men, it will come to nought: but if it be of God, ye cannot overthrow it; lest haply ye be found even to fight against God.

All Gamaliel was saying here is that if these are servants of God that you are fighting, then you are actually fighting God Himself. And since you do not know for sure, it might be in your best interest to leave them alone. I know many people reading this will be thinking, *I have never persecuted or gossiped about any man of God*, but this form of rebellion can come out in more subtle ways.

Do you realise that you can actually undermine the authority of God by failing to recognise and discern when God is ministering through His servant? Let me explain. This is what happened when the Lord Jesus arrived in His hometown of Galilee. The Bible says that "He could do no mighty work there." Why? Instead of recognising Him as the Messiah, all the people could see was Jesus who grew up two houses down the road whose father was a tradesman that used to repair their furniture.

They hindered the move of the Spirit by their familiarity. The same Jesus who had raised the dead, opened blind eyes, and healed leprosy was reduced to healing a few headaches.

Mark 6:5
And He could there do no mighty work, save that He laid his hands upon a few sick folk, and healed them.

Now notice here the Bible does not say that He would not do any mighty works. It says that He could not do it. In other words, He tried and failed. I mean Jesus Christ of Nazareth, could do no mighty work there. That is how much they grieved the Spirit of God.

Do you realise that when a preacher is ministering, you do not respond to encourage the preacher? Oh, no! You should be shouting amen to agree with the Word of God you are receiving. Some of you who are ministers will testify that no matter how excited you are about the Word, when you try to minister to a crowd that is unresponsive, it's as if someone has just poured water on the fire that was in your spirit. That is because they really have poured water on the fire of the Spirit.

I said it before, and I'll say it again: God is a God of order, and it's time for the Church to grow up and get in line with that. The Bible commands us to speak the truth in love.

Ephesians 4:15
But speaking the truth in love, may grow up into him in all things, which is the head, even Christ.

If I am required to speak the truth in the spirit of love, then you also need to receive it in that same spirit knowing that what is being said is in your own best interest. That's part of growing up. If a person is drowning, the lifeguard cannot afford to take the time to tie a ribbon around the life preserver and make it look pretty before throwing it out there. What matters most is getting the life preserver to the one whose life is in danger. Many Christians don't realise they are drowning in the same water that is being used to quench the Holy Spirit's fire. Some of you may not like some of the things that have been said in this chapter but understand, while it may not look pretty, they're there to save your life.

Speaking the truth in love does not mean speaking in sugary sweet tones to communicate the truth to you. I am not Mary Poppins, and you should not need a spoonful of sugar to make the medicine go down. Of course, we always want to make sure that our words are "always with grace" as the Bible says. The fact remains, speaking the truth can sometimes be unpleasant, even offensive. But I would rather hurt your feelings for a brief moment so that you will not hurt the Holy Spirit's feelings and cause Him to retreat and be silent. I'd rather you be corrected and preserve your fellowship with Him.

If I love you, and I do, I am compelled to tell you the truth about what the Word of God is saying concerning grieving and quenching the Spirit of God by being unruly. It is dangerous to be in danger, but it is more dangerous to be in danger and not even know it. This is what is happening to many Christians today. They are quenching the Spirit of God and are not even aware of it. If I know there is a fire in a building, and you don't, and I know the way out to safety, and you don't, I want to make sure you know that there is a fire and that you hear me clearly when I tell you where the fire exit is. Honouring God by honouring men and women of God is the way out of danger.

The Scripture says:

Proverbs 25:28
He that hath no rule over his own spirit is like a city that is broken down, and without walls.

Just look at the picture being painted there. It is showing us that the lack of self-control will put us in a dangerous state. And there's nothing more dangerous than quenching the Holy Spirit and silencing His voice. What I have shared with you concerning those that are unruly, those who are breaking rank, are not suggestions; they are warnings, and warnings are only necessary when danger is present and protection or preservation is needed. The only appropriate action to take if you are unruly is to rule your spirit. Get back in line with God's order by walking in love. That requires exercising that component of love called self-control. Self-control is not only about restraining yourself from doing what's wrong; it is also about constraining yourself to do what's right. It is allowing the Spirit of love to influence the decisions you make to show honour.

You cannot fight a man or woman of God without fighting God Himself, and you can't fight God and win. To borrow a phrase coined by author, poet, and activist James Weldon Johnson, your arm's too short to box with God. Remember, God honours men and women of God. If God honours them enough to place them in the positions or offices they are in, who are you not to honour them? Honour is everything! If you can't honour the man, honour the office, and if you can't honour the office, honour the God who created the office. Recognise that behind every genuine man and woman of God there is the God who made them so.

CHAPTER SIX

Comfort the Feebleminded

An amazing revelation of the Holy Spirit and how we can partner with Him is hidden in these three little words,

"comfort the feebleminded."

At first glance, you may be wondering what comfort has to do with the feebleminded, and what any of that has to do with the Holy Spirit. By the time you finish reading this chapter, you will understand the connection. As you read on, pay close attention to how peace, a component of the fruit of the Spirit, is necessary for carrying out this instruction. As in other chapters, I will take the time to break down the words to their meaning based on the original language. Then we can move from there to see what it is we are being instructed to do in order to maintain our fellowship with the Holy Spirit, and how to do it.

Now, in 1 Thessalonians 5:14, the word 'feebleminded' is a translation of the Greek word *oligopsuchous*. In certain translations, it is rendered 'fainthearted.' To be feebleminded in this sense does not refer specifically to stupidity. Rather, it refers to weakness of will and vacillation or wavering of mind. In the Septuagint (which is the Greek translation of the Old Testament from the original Hebrew), *kashal* (or *koshel*) is used as the equivalent carrying the meaning of tottering or feeble-kneed (see **Isaiah 35:3**). The imagery is of someone who is leaning this way and that, unable to stand on their own.

With that understanding in mind, when we talk about the feebleminded, we are talking about those who are weak-minded and can be convinced by anything. Feebleminded people have no power to influence, and they can be influenced by anything. Comforting the feebleminded is a ministry appointed by the Holy Ghost to every Christian. We each have a unique opportunity to partner with the Holy Spirit who is the Comforter. This requires that we get a better understanding of who He is and how He carries out this aspect of His ministry.

The word 'comfort' in 1 Thessalonians 5:14 is translated from the Greek word *paramythéomai* which means 'to speak to or address by way of admonition or incentive' or 'to calm and console.' The words you speak become very important in this ministry of comforting the feeble minded. As you walk with the Spirit in love, you become a carrier of His peace, and what you say communicates the peace of God to others so the instruction here is to bring coherence to the spirit, soul and body of our feebleminded Christian brothers and sisters.

Galatians 5:22-23
But the fruit of the Spirit is love, joy, peace, longsuffering, gentleness, goodness, faith, meekness, temperance: against such there is no law.

As I said before, the problem of the feebleminded is that they are weak-minded, and as a result, they are easily influenced. They have not yet developed enough spiritual maturity and tenacity to withstand the pressures and influences of wrong teaching. Ephesians 4:14 says that such ones are like children, tossed to and fro by every wind of doctrine. When Prophet So-and-so comes to town, they run after that one and follow his teaching. Then when Apostle so-and-so comes through, they run after him and switch to his teaching. The feebleminded are influenced by every new teaching they hear and are unable to distinguish between truth and counterfeit.

So, the Bible lets us know that gifts have been given in order to address this issue. Watch what the Bible says:

Ephesians 4:7-8, 14
7 But unto every one of us is given grace according to the measure of the gift of Christ. 8 Wherefore he saith, When He ascended up on high, He led captivity captive, and gave gifts unto men... 14 That we henceforth be no more children, tossed to and fro, and carried about with every wind of doctrine, by the sleight of men, and cunning craftiness, whereby they lie in wait to deceive.

If you read this passage in its entirety, you will see that it is referring to the gifts which the Lord Jesus Christ gave to the Body of Christ so that we can mature in the things of the Lord. Among those gifts are what we call the five-fold ministry: apostles, prophets, evangelists, pastors and teachers (Ephesians 4:11). But the gifts which Christ has given are not limited to the five-fold ministry gifts. In fact, the first gift which He gave to the Body of Christ after salvation is the Person of the Holy Spirit.

There are several scriptures which either directly or indirectly refer to the Holy Spirit as a gift. Jesus Himself says, "And I will pray the Father, and He shall give you another Comforter, that He may abide with you forever." He was referring to the Holy Spirit who was given (or gifted) to us. Also, in Luke's account of the Gospel, Jesus made it clear that the Holy Spirit is a gift. Watch what the Bible says:

Luke 11:11-13
11 If a son shall ask bread of any of you that is a father, will he give him a stone? or if he ask a fish, will he for a fish give him a

serpent? 12 Or if he shall ask an egg, will he offer him a scorpion? 13 *If ye then, being evil, know how to give good gifts unto your children: how much more shall your heavenly Father give the Holy Spirit to them that ask him?* **[emphasis added]**

Right there, Jesus clearly makes a parallel comparison between the good gifts that earthly fathers give to their children and the good Gift of the Holy Spirit that our heavenly Father gives to His children. The Holy Spirit is a Gift, and He also was given so that "we henceforth be no more children, tossed to and fro, and carried about with every wind of doctrine." One of the ways He accomplishes this is through His ministry as Comforter.

To better understand this ministry, let's go back and look at what Jesus said of the Holy Spirit when He was first introducing Him to His disciples:

John 14:16
And I will pray the Father, and He shall give you another Comforter, that He may abide with you forever.

For you to get what is being communicated right here, it's essential for you to understand the context of this introduction. Jesus had been walking, talking, eating, teaching, living, and fellowshipping with His disciples for three years, night and day. Now He was returning to the Father and would no longer be with them physically. You can imagine how close the disciples must have felt to Jesus after having walked with Him for three years. They had developed and inseparable bond. He had always been with them during that time, but now He was leaving. Jesus, knowing how difficult His leaving would be for them, carries out His own ministry as Comforter and introduces the Holy Spirit as "another Comforter," *allos Paraklétos*.

The Greek word *allos* translated 'another' means 'another of the same kind.' Notice Jesus did not say the Holy Spirit is *heteros Paraklétos*, another of a different kind, but *allos* which means He is another who is exactly like Jesus. As the Comforter (*Parakletos*), the Holy Spirit is the One who comes alongside us to help us. Just as Jesus walked alongside His disciples, now the Holy Spirit is being introduced as the One who will come alongside them and help them.

As you read on a little further, you will see exactly why Jesus introduces the Holy Spirit as another Comforter. He says:

John 14:18
I will not leave you comfortless: I will come to you.

I don't want you to miss what He is talking about right here. In the previous chapters starting from around chapter 13, Jesus was telling His disciples that He was going to leave them. After saying that, He now says, "I will come to you." What Jesus is saying right there is that He was leaving, but He would come to them through the manifestation of One who is exactly like Himself, *allos Parakletos*, the Holy Spirit. And it is through the ministry of the Comforter, the Holy Spirit, that He (Jesus) would not leave them comfortless.

Now, to better understand this ministry of the Comforter, let's take a look at that same verse in the Amplified version:

John 14:18
I will not leave you as orphans [comfortless, desolate, bereaved, forlorn, helpless]; I will come [back] to you.

From this we can see that when Jesus says, "I will not leave you comfortless," He is saying, "I will not leave you as orphans." This word 'orphan' comes from the Greek word *orphanós* which means those bereft of a teacher, guide, or guardian. It is precisely this ministry of the Comforter that the feebleminded need. The only way the feebleminded cannot be "tossed to and fro, and carried about with every wind of doctrine, by the sleight of men, and cunning craftiness, whereby they lie in wait to deceive" is if they have someone to teach, guide, and take over guardianship of them. This is the ministry of the Comforter: teacher, guide, and guardian.

As the Comforter—*allos Paraklétos*—the Holy Spirit comes alongside us to teach, guide, and provide guardianship. Now, the duty of a guardian is to take care of and protect a person who cannot take care of himself or herself, such as a child whose parents have died. We can now see the connection between Jesus not leaving us comfortless as orphans and the ministry of the Holy Spirit as our Comforter. His ministry is what brings the kind of comfort spoken of in 1 Thessalonians 5:14 where it says, "comfort the feebleminded." Remember, I said that the word for 'comfort' there is *paramythéomai*, which means to speak to or address someone, whether by way of admonition or incentive, or to calm and console. When a feebleminded person is under guardianship and correctly taught and guided, his or her mind becomes calm and settled.

James paints the picture of what happens when a person's mind is unsettled like this:

James 1:8
A double-minded man is unstable in all his ways.

While the context of this verse is dealing with faith, the principle still applies. We often miss the fullness of what the Scripture is saying because we only take a glance at it and do not take the time to meditate and allow the Holy Spirit to give us greater revelation. A double-minded man is one who goes to and fro in his mind. In other words, he wavers in his mind. One minute he believes one thing, the next minute he believes something else. We could actually say the same thing about those who are "tossed to and fro and carried about with every wind of doctrine." They waver in their minds which causes them to become unstable. But if through correct teaching and guidance a person becomes no longer double-minded, his ways will no longer be unstable. In other words, instead of being feebleminded and unstable, he becomes calm and settled in his mind and the result is peace.

Having seen how the ministry of the Comforter operates, we can now better understand the opportunity to partner with Him in this area. The question is, how do you partner with Him? The first thing you must realise is you cannot give what you do not have. Before you can bring comfort to the feebleminded, you must be first partaker of it. Apostle Paul says:

2 Corinthians 1:3-4
Blessed be God, even the Father of our Lord Jesus Christ, the Father of mercies, and the God of all comfort; 4 Who comforteth us in all our tribulation, that we may be able to comfort them which are in any trouble, by the comfort wherewith we ourselves are comforted of God.

What Paul is saying is that God comforts us in all our trouble so that we can comfort other people who are in trouble. We offer the same comfort that we ourselves received. That means that the first feebleminded person the Holy Spirit wants to comfort is you.

One weak-minded person cannot bring comfort to another weak-minded person. That would be like the blind leading the blind, or in this case, one tottering and feeble-kneed person leaning on another tottering and feeble-kneed person. Both of you will topple over. First, submit yourself to the guardianship of the Holy Spirit by walking with Him in love and allowing Him to teach and guide you.

Comfort the Feebleminded

Then you will be able to give of what you have received to others.

Walking in the Spirit is walking in love, and one of the manifestations of love is peace, *eiréné*, which means peace of mind. By providing teaching and guidance, we bring peace to the feebleminded. There is no better comfort for the feebleminded than peace, calmness of mind. This intensifies the necessity for us to maintain fellowship with the Holy Spirit and not quench His fire. Understand that He is the Comforter, and your cooperation with Him is seen in how you also comfort and strengthen those who are weak and feeble in their walk with the Lord.

It is the responsibility of every christian to comfort those who are troubled in mind or fainthearted and help them to keep going strong in the faith. Every single person that is born again and has the Holy Spirit living on the inside of them bears that responsibility. The Bible tells us that He has given us the ministry of reconciliation:

2 Corinthians 5:17-18
Therefore if any man be in Christ, he is a new creature: old things are passed away; behold, all things are become new. And all things are of God, who hath reconciled us to himself by Jesus Christ, and hath given to us the ministry of reconciliation.

Many christians make the mistake of thinking that only those within the five-fold ministry have the responsibility to minister to those who are in anguish of spirit. Yet all the ministry gifts are given by the Holy Ghost to equip the saints for the work of the ministry. Watch what the scripture says:

Ephesians 4:11-12
And He gave some, apostles; and some, prophets; and some, evangelists; and some, pastors and teachers; For the perfecting of the saints, for the work of the ministry, for the edifying of the Body of Christ.

This is a call that everyone must answer, and when you neglect this duty you quench the fire of the Spirit in your life. Apostle Paul said something important when he was talking about the call of God upon his life. He said:

Galatians 1:15-16
But when it pleased God, who separated me from my mother's womb, and called me by His grace, to reveal His Son in me, that I might preach Him among the heathen.

Paul said I was called to reveal Jesus. When you comfort and strengthen the feebleminded, you also are revealing and manifesting the character and personality of this same Jesus by His Spirit. On the other hand, when you neglect this calling you actually stifle and choke the Spirit of God and stop Him from working in your life.

CHAPTER SEVEN

Support the Weak

Most people think meekness is weakness, but that belief is a gross misunderstanding of what meekness is all about. You have to understand that I am here starting with a recap of meekness not because we are repeating the topic but because supporting the weak which we are rightly dealing with in this chapter requires meekness to be established as a prerequisite so in this chapter it is imperative that I show you how the component of the fruit of the Spirit called meekness gives us the ability to support the weak.

It might seem we are taking the long route to arrive at our destination of supporting the weak but its necessary to cover all basis before we delve into the subject matter of this chapter which is supporting the weak. Now, Miriam and Aaron did not understand meekness which is why they rose against Moses for marrying an Ethiopian woman. Their mistake teaches us a valuable lesson about meekness, what it is and how we can employ it in supporting the weak. Let's see what happened from the book of Numbers:

Numbers 12:1
And Miriam and Aaron spake against Moses because of the Ethiopian woman whom he had married: for he had married an Ethiopian woman.

Miriam and Aaron mistook Moses' meekness for weakness, when in fact, it was one of his greatest strengths. Watch what the Scripture says of Moses:

Numbers 12:3
(Now the man Moses was very meek, above all the men which were upon the face of the earth.)

Now Moses had great power because He was a friend of God. He recognised that any power he had was a direct result of his friendship and interactions with God. He had learned to exercise that power with restraint for the benefit of God's people, but he was not always this way. This is the same Moses who used his power at one time to destroy someone else.

Lessons in Meekness

You see, Moses grew up in the household of Pharaoh, the most powerful man in all of Egypt. He was raised in the royal courts and grew up in a position of privilege and power. And then one day, when he was grown, He went out to where his fellow Hebrew brothers were labouring as slaves, and then something happened that would change the course of his life forever. Look at what the Bible says:

Exodus 2:11-12
And it came to pass in those days, when Moses was grown, that he went out unto his brethren, and looked on their burdens: and he spied an Egyptian smiting an Hebrew, one of his brethren. And he looked this way and that way, and when he saw that there was no man, he slew the Egyptian, and hid him in the sand.

This Egyptian had been abusing his power by beating one of the Hebrews who was already suffering under the weight of slavery and hard labour. Unfortunately, Moses thought he could follow suit. So, when he saw the Egyptian bullying the Hebrew slave, he beat this Egyptian to death. Not only that, but he then dug a hole in the sand and hid the dead body in it. Make no mistake about it,

Support the Weak

Moses had the power of position as well as physical. But in this instance, he used his power wrongly.

Immediately after that, Moses escaped and went to live in a place called Midian. One day, as he was sitting down at a well, he found himself in yet another encounter with bullies. This time it was some shepherds. Watch what the Bible says:

Exodus 2:15-17
15 Now when Pharaoh heard this thing, he sought to slay Moses. But Moses fled from the face of Pharaoh, and dwelt in the land of Midian: and he sat down by a well. 16 Now the priest of Midian had seven daughters: and they came and drew water, and filled the troughs to water their father's flock. 17 And the shepherds came and drove them away: but Moses stood up and helped them, and watered their flock.

What Moses did not realise is that when he ran away from Egypt, he was running to school in Midian. You see, pain will teach you a lesson that pride prevented you from learning. Pain will put you in the school that pride expelled you from. And Moses, who after killing the Egyptian and running away from everything that he had once known, was now in Midian learning lessons on how to be meek.

These are lessons we also must learn. When power is misused or abused, we will face hard lessons in strange places. But when power is used to help, deliver, and restore, God will see to it that we are rewarded. Just look at what happened to Moses:

Exodus 2:18-22
18 And when they came to Reuel their father, he said, 'How is it that ye are come so soon to day?' 19 And they said, 'An Egyptian delivered us out of the hand of the shepherds, and also drew water enough for us, and watered the flock.' 20 And he said unto

his daughters, 'And where is he? Why is it that ye have left the man? Call him, that he may eat bread.' 21 And Moses was content to dwell with the man: and he gave Moses Zipporah his daughter. 22 And she bare him a son, and he called his name Gershom: for he said, I have been a stranger in a strange land.

Let me remind you, Moses was not weak by any stretch of the imagination. He was no wimp. He chased away the shepherds who had been harassing the daughters of the Midianite priest, but this time he did not kill any of them. Whereas he had abused his power back in Egypt, in Midian, he learned to exercise that power under control.

Jesus Our Example of Meekness

Many Christians in the Body of Christ, especially leaders, struggle with this. They have power, but they do not exercise restraint and therefore abuse it. When a situation occurs involving weakness, they are not mature enough to know the difference between using their power to harm or to help. Consequently, instead of walking in a spirit of meekness, they become spiritual bullies beating up those who they see as weak. The Bible says that we must "support the weak," not bully them. And this is not how we have learned Christ.

There is no one greater and more powerful than Jesus. As powerful as He is, He is the premier role model for meekness. In the Old Testament, the prophet Zechariah declared of Jesus:

Zechariah 9:9
Rejoice greatly, O daughter of Zion; shout, O daughter of Jerusalem: behold, thy King cometh unto thee: he is just, and having salvation; *lowly* [emphasis added], and riding upon an ass, and upon a colt the foal of an ass.

Jesus is described as "lowly" by Zechariah. And in Matthew, Jesus describing himself refers to the same Old Testament scripture giving us an even clearer understanding. He says:

Matthew 21:4-5
All this was done, that it might be fulfilled which was spoken by the prophet, saying, "Tell ye the daughter of Sion, Behold, thy King cometh unto thee, *meek* [emphasis added], and sitting upon an ass, and a colt the foal of an ass."

Notice the dynamic of power. He comes as a king, and at the same time, He comes meekly. Some might see this as an oxymoron because they cannot reconcile power and meekness. But I can assure you, there is no contradiction here. Anywhere in the world, a king is identified with great power. It's interesting that many in the Church want to be known for the demonstration of power, but not many want to be known for meekness which is one of the greatest demonstrations of power.

This is not the first time Jesus referred to himself as meek. Ten chapters earlier, He says this:

Matthew 11:29
Take My yoke upon you, and learn of Me; for I am meek and lowly in heart: and ye shall find rest unto your souls.

There is something that most Christians miss when reading this passage. They catch the "take My yoke upon you" part (though many may not understand what that means). They may even catch the "I am meek and lowly" and "ye shall find rest unto your souls" parts. But often they miss the part that says, "learn of Me." What is it that Jesus wants us to learn from Him? The next phrase gives us a clue: "for I am meek and lowly in heart." You see, meekness does not come automatically. It is something that is learned and practiced. A yoke is an instrument of apprenticeship; we are yoked with or alongside the Master so that we can learn of Him. One of the things He desires for us to learn is to be meek as He is meek. Only then can we "support the weak."

Strength to Support

Now, we need to understand something of the etymology of these words, "support the weak." The word 'weak' is the Greek word, *asthenés*, which means to be 'without adequate strength.' It is the negation of the word *sthenóō* which means 'strengthened.' When a person is weak, they do not have the strength to do what they want to do or are supposed to do. It is possible for a christian to be weak in body, weak in faith, weak in knowledge, even weak in character. In the Body of Christ, we all have value. Christ died for all of us. But we are not all the same. As christians, we all have access to the same spiritual resources, but there are some who are stronger spiritually, or as some would say, more powerful. This is not because they are more anointed but because they are more spiritually mature with greater grace and understanding. It is to such ones that Paul would give the instruction, "support the weak."

As I pointed out in the previous chapter, the feebleminded can only be comforted by those who are not functioning on the same feebleminded level as they are. Likewise, the weak cannot be supported by those who are spiritually weak. That kind of support can only come from those who are more spiritually mature. What kind of support am I talking about? Let's take a closer look.

The word 'support' right there is the Greek word *antéchomai*. This word means, 'keep hold of them, to help them on;' or 'to keep one's self directly opposite to anyone.' *Antéchomai* is derived from two words, *anti* (against) and *echo* (hold). So, the most literal translation would be to 'hold against.' When you think of how we use the word 'support' in everyday language, it will make sense. You can support someone emotionally by holding your strong emotions against their weak emotions to help them on. You can support someone or something physically. For example, if you sit on a chair for support, then the chair is being used to hold against the weight that it is supporting. Let me use another example.

One of my companies deals with building construction. There are times on our larger project sites when we have to use large cranes to move equipment or supplies from one site location to another. These cranes are powerful and are capable of supporting tons of weight. The hook and the chains of the crane hold against the weight that is being transported from one place to another.

We can see how it works when we're talking about support using a chair or even a crane. But what does it mean to support the weak? To put it in literal terms, how do we 'hold against' the weak? The answer is, the same way Moses did when he delivered the daughters of the Midianite priest: by exercising power under restraint. Let me explain it another way.

Some time ago, I started working out with a personal trainer. He had me doing all kinds of things to get my body into better shape. Some things I didn't like doing. Other things I didn't like doing even more (and still don't, like eating those ungodly meals of chicken breast and brown rice). But as the saying goes, no pain, no gain. So, the trainer would come to my house, and we would do some gym routines. Now, I'm no weakling to start. I'm a second-degree black belt in martial arts, so I already could do a few things here and there. But my personal trainer's job among other things is to spot me during weight training so that if I make the mistake of lifting something that is too heavy for me to manage on my own, he can provide the support necessary to prevent me from injuring myself.

Now, as much as my teenage son might want to develop his muscles and be strong like his dad, I know that he is not yet at a level where he can support the same kind of weight that I can. It would be dangerous for him to try to lift a weight that he's not strong enough to lift. At the same time, it would be careless of me to stand by and watch him struggle under that weight without doing something about it. He could be crushed if his arms gave way. But because I love him, and I have more strength or power than he does, I make it my duty to spot him. That way, if he because of his weakness gets under something that he can't manage on his own, I can support that weight and make sure that my son does not injure himself.

Because of spiritual immaturity or weakness, Christians can sometimes get into weighty situations that if left unsupported can crush or destroy them. That is why Apostle Paul tells us:

Romans 15:1
We then that are strong ought to bear the infirmities of the weak, and not to please ourselves.

This is what we ought to do; it is necessary and desirable. If you are strong, your strength is not just for you, but also for the benefit of those who are weak.

A similar instruction is given by the Apostle Paul in Galatians 6:1 where he says:

Brethren, if a man be overtaken in a fault, ye which are spiritual, restore such an one in the spirit of meekness...

As I said before, there are times when Christians are weak, and they end up in situations that are too weighty for them to manage. In this verse, Paul says that they can be "overtaken in a fault." Think of it like a weaker person who thinks he can lift a certain weight in the gym only to find out that it was more than he bargained for. He does not have adequate strength to support it on his own. Now this is where some Christians, especially those in leadership, miss it. If someone messes up and is under a weight that has the potential to crush or destroy them, that is not the time to point out how weak they are, and how powerful you are, no! That is not what love does.

Love restores in the spirit of meekness—power with restraint or under the Spirit's control. The loving thing to do is to use that power to help provide support for the one who is weak. The key word there is "overtaken." It carries with it the sense of one who is caught by surprise in a fault because of his ignorance, inattention, or the stress of temptation. He is caught in a moment of weakness. Such a person needs support. This is not always an easy thing to do, and I know first-hand how difficult it can be. Let me give you an example of what I'm talking about.

Gaining the Weak

There was a time when a certain man of God levelled a serious accusation against me. Based on the relationship we had, it was the worst thing he could have said about me. I thought this person knew me very well or at least understood my character. I loved and still love this person dearly. But in that moment, faced with such an appalling accusation, I identified with David when he said:

Psalm 41:9
Yea, mine own familiar friend, in whom I trusted, which did eat of my bread, hath lifted up his heel against me.

I know right there some of you are trying to figure out who it is I'm talking about, but don't worry about it. You don't know him, and

I'm not about to tell you who it is. You don't need to know. All you need to know is that the accusation was staggering, and I knew it would carry serious repercussions. This man was so sure that he was right, and he had so much anger, I was beyond shocked!

The challenging part for me was knowing that I had indisputable evidence which, had it been used against him, would have proven the accusation false beyond any shadow of a doubt. But that is not what the Spirit of love wanted me to do at that time. It would have dishonoured the anointing on this man's life and grieved the Spirit of God. So, instead of using my power against him, which might have devastated him and harmed his ministry, I chose to walk in love, hold my peace, and demonstrate the power of meekness.

Sometimes meekness requires us to speak and act; sometimes it requires us to keep our mouths shut and be still. Did doing what I did make me weak? No, it did not. It may have made me look weak to some, but in fact, it made me stronger. I maintained and strengthened my fellowship with the Holy Spirit and left space for Him to deal with the man's heart without me getting in the way. Paul understood this when he wrote:

1 Corinthians 9:22
To the weak became I as weak, that I might gain the weak…

Notice, he said he became "as weak." Even though he was not weak, his actions may have appeared that way to some. Paul realised, as should we, that while meekness may prove to be challenging at times, the end justifies the means: "that I might gain the weak."

You see in order to help the weak we need to be meek. This is the easiest of chapters because we have already dealt with understanding meekness which literally mean to have a teachable spirit!

Power Belongs to God

I did not share my experience to justify anyone's belief that meekness is only for when a person is "overtaken" in a fault. That is not the case. Meekness is par for the course every day since that is what the Holy Spirit demonstrates toward us daily. The Bible declares:

Psalm 62:11
God hath spoken once; twice have I heard this; that power belongeth unto God.

The Holy Spirit is not just like God. He is God, He possesses the attributes of God, and scripture bears this out. He is *omnipresent*: Psalm 139:7-8 (present everywhere); John 14:17 (present in every christian). He is *omniscient* (knows all things): Isaiah 40:13; 1 Corinthians 2:9-11; John 16 v.13, John 14:26 (He cannot teach all things unless He knows all things, and He cannot guide us into all truth unless He knows all truth. He is *sovereign*: Isaiah 40:13. He is *omnipotent* (He has infinite power): Luke 1:35; Romans 8:11; Zechariah 4:6. He is *eternal:* Hebrews 9:14; John 14:16 (He will abide with us forever). He is *Creator* (involved in creation): Genesis 1:1-2, 26; 2:7 (compare with Job 33:4); Job 26:13 (see also Psalm 19:1). He is *holy:* Romans 1:4. He is *good:* Psalm 143:10 (compare with Luke 18:19 and Mark 10:18. He is *allos माraklétos* (another Comforter, another of the same kind/genus): John 14:16. All of these attributes of the Holy Spirit identify Him as part of the triune godhead.

Since the Holy Spirit is God, what is the practical application of His deity for us as christians? Why is it so important for us to know He is God? If He is God (and He is), He is not the servant of the Church, but the Lord of the Church. If He is God (and He is), He is not here to do our bidding; we are here to do His bidding. If He is God (and He is), He is not here to please us; we are here to please Him. If

He is God (and He is), He is not here to be your cheerleader for worship; He is One who should be worshiped, praised and adored. Everything we ascribe to God, we can ascribe to Him because He is God. Therefore, being God, He is the source of all power because "power belongs to God."

The Holy Spirit is all powerful, yet He "spots" us when we are weak. He does not use His power to bully us or beat us up when we mess up. Instead, He uses His power to support us in our weakness and to help us escape danger. As powerful as He is, the Holy Spirit chooses to demonstrate meekness, just like Jesus. He is a shining example of power under control, and He demonstrates that aspect of His love towards us every day. If we are going to walk with the Holy Spirit in love, then we must also do the same for others who are weak as He does for us.

CHAPTER EIGHT

Be Patient Toward All Men

I used to think that I was a patient person. Then I got married. It immediately became apparent that I was a little less patient than I previously thought. Then the children came, and they completely cured me of any grand delusions I had about ever having the patience of a saint!

It is said that patience is a virtue, a quality that is good for a person to have. It is a component of the fruit of the Spirit that is well-known but not well understood. In this chapter, we will speak primarily of patience since that is the virtue we are required to employ in carrying out the instruction, "be patient toward all men." It is important to note, however, that patience works together with another component of the fruit of the Spirit called kindness. As we go through the scriptures, I will show you how the one is complementary to the other.

Galatians 5:22-23
But the fruit of the Spirit is love, joy, peace, longsuffering, gentleness, goodness, faith, meekness, temperance: against such there is no law.

Patience is not a dominant virtue in most people. If you doubt it, the next time you're near a queue that is moving a little slowly, pay attention to the annoyed expressions and frustrated grumblings of the people around you. To bring it closer to home, remember the last time you waited for something. Most of us don't even want to wait for a microwave which takes mere seconds to heat up some food.

One thing I've learned in my fellowship with the Holy Spirit is that He never wastes words. If He through the Apostle Paul tells us we must be patient with everyone, it is because that is something we need to hear, know and do. Now I know that word 'patient' there confuses many people; the King James rendering of the Bible does not tell even half the story of what that word means. Consequently, when Paul says that we are to be patient toward all men, many miss it. So, let's take a few moments to get some understanding about exactly what is being communicated.

Big Fire

The word translated as 'patient' is *makrothyméō* in the Greek. It is a combination of two words *makro* which means big or long, and *thymeo* (or *thumos*) which means fire or burning. Have you ever heard of expressions like, "getting fired up" or "burning with anger?" They give the sense of being inflamed or having very strong feelings such as anger or excitement. That's *thumos*. If we took the literal translation into the English, what Paul was saying is, *be big or long fire toward all men*. To help you understand what I'm talking about, allow me to introduce you to Mama Ann.

Mama Ann is someone the Bible refers to as "a widow indeed." She's a godly woman known for the good she does for others. One of the things she's known most for is holding men and women of God in high honour. These are some of the reasons I appreciate her so much. Some time ago, I made up my mind to be a blessing to her. Mama Ann does not lack much of anything. She is well cared for. But I found out she loves candles; so every year I look for the best and most fragrant candles I can find and give it to her as a gift. I'm not talking about anything you could pick up at the Poundshop. We go for quality, and the better the quality, the more expensive it is.

Be Patient Toward All Men

One of the things I discovered about expensive candles is that it all comes down to how well it burns. The best candles release high-quality fragrance without filling the place with smoke. Most importantly, they burn for a long time. It will take an extremely long time for a flame of fire to burn through the wick of a high-quality candle. That is what the kind of patience (*makrothyméō*) Apostle Paul is talking about here is like: an expensive candle that has "long fire." It takes a long time to burn, it doesn't fill the room with the smoke of unkindness, and all the while, it emits the highest quality fragrance: love.

On that day as the Holy Spirit sat opposite me in my room he said: "This word *makrothyméō* is different from the other Greek word translated as 'patient' in the New Testament which is *hupomoné*, which means steadfastness or endurance."

Watch the scripture he gave me to prove it:

James 1:4
But let patience [*hupomoné*] have her perfect work, that ye may be perfect and entire, wanting nothing.

If you are like some of my kindred from the motherland, you understand that waiting and patience mean something very different from other parts of the world. I know I have witnesses out there, but don't worry your secret is safe. Being patient in Africa does not mean it will come in an hour or a day. That thing you are waiting for may not even come at all! This is not the big or long fire kind of patience Paul is talking about in 1 Thessalonians 5. *Makrothyméō* is not talking about you waiting patiently somewhere. It is an entirely different kind of patience altogether. To explain, let me give you another example of how this *makrothyméō*—big fire—patience is used in the Scripture.

Hello Holy Spirit

In the book of Hebrews, we also see the word *makrothyméō* connected to the subject of faith. The Scripture says:

Hebrews 6:12
That ye be not slothful, but followers of them who through faith and patience [*makrothyméō*] inherit the promises.

This verse says faith plus this type of patience brings you through. This *makrothyméō* is the ability to withstand assaults, attacks, trials, temptations, or whatever the devil throws at you. It means to stand in heat, to stand in cold, to stand in trials, to stand in problems, all the while maintaining the same stand without wavering one moment. This *makrothyméō*, this remarkable form of patience, can make you go forth like a ramrod against every force that comes against you. It's like going through a battlefield, bombs falling on your right and on your left with landmines all around, yet this makrothyméō causes you to go in and come out without your being affected one bit. It's that patience which brings you through like Meshach, Shadrach, and Abednego coming out from the fiery furnace without even the smell of smoke on them. There is a parable in the Bible that speaks of the power of this kind of *makrothyméō* patience, but many have missed it. Watch what the Bible says:

Matthew 18:21-35
21 Then came Peter to him, and said, "Lord, how oft shall my brother sin against me, and I forgive him? Till seven times?" 22 Jesus saith unto him, "I say not unto thee, until seven times: but, until seventy times seven. 23 Therefore is the Kingdom of Heaven likened unto a certain king, which would take account of his servants. 24 And when he had begun to reckon, one was brought unto him, which owed him ten thousand talents. 25 But forasmuch as he had not to pay, his lord commanded him to be sold, and his wife, and children, and all that he had, and payment

to be made. 26 The servant therefore fell down, and worshipped him, saying, 'Lord, have patience with me, and I will pay thee all.' 27 Then the lord of that servant was moved with compassion, and loosed him, and forgave him the debt. 28 But the same servant went out, and found one of his fellow servants, which owed him an hundred pence: and he laid hands on him, and took him by the throat, saying, 'Pay me that thou owest.' 29 And his fellow servant fell down at his feet, and besought him, saying, 'Have patience with me, and I will pay thee all.' 30 And he would not: but went and cast him into prison, till he should pay the debt. 31 So when his fellow servants saw what was done, they were very sorry, and came and told unto their lord all that was done. 32 Then his lord, after that he had called him, said unto him, 'O thou wicked servant, I forgave thee all that debt, because thou desiredst me: 33 Shouldest not thou also have had compassion on thy fellow servant, even as I had pity on thee? '34 And his lord was wroth, and delivered him to the tormentors, till he should pay all that was due unto him. 35 So likewise shall my heavenly Father do also unto you, if ye from your hearts forgive not every one his brother their trespasses."

I know that this is a relatively lengthy passage of Scripture, but I want you to get the whole picture so that you can see the crucial point that is often overlooked. (I also know that if I only give you the scripture reference, some of you will never pick up a Bible and look it up. So, I'm covering both bases.) When most christians read this scripture, they understand from the opening and closing verses that it is referring primarily to the subject of forgiveness. But let's take a closer look.

The servant in this parable owed the king what would be equivalent to millions of pounds. Being a servant, there was no way in the world this man could repay that debt. In our times, if you owe a large debt to the government, they are within their rights to come and take all of your possessions and sell them to pay off the debt. But in those times, if a man could not repay his debt, they would sell all the possessions along with the man, his wife, and his children too!

I want you to see what happens here. Knowing that this man could never pay this debt, the Bible says:

Matthew 18:26
The servant therefore fell down, and worshipped him, saying, "Lord, have patience with me, and I will pay thee all."

This is where we miss it. We read the text and assume the servant was asking for forgiveness, but the servant said:

Lord, have patience [*makrothyméō*] with me, and I will pay thee all.

He didn't ask for more time or the cancellation of debt. He asked for patience. And the king's response to that request is an example of what Paul means when he says, "be patient toward all men." Look at what it says:

Matthew 18:27
Then the lord of that servant was moved with compassion, and loosed him, and forgave him the debt.

The lord of the servant was moved in his *splankna*: his innermost being, his very intestines were moved to show kindness to this servant. But then something interesting happens.

This same servant who received the cancellation of his entire debt goes out and meets someone who owes him a few thousand dollars. Watch what the Bible says:

Matthew 18:29
And his fellow servant fell down at his feet, and besought him, saying, "Have patience [*makrothyméō*] with me, and I will pay thee all."

Here the fellow servant, someone in the same position as him who had the same need he once had, makes the same request that the servant made of the king: "have patience with me." But instead of responding in love and kindness as his lord had done for him, the servant throws his fellow servant into prison. When the lord found out what his servant who had been released from his debt had done, he called him wicked which is literally translated evil, and delivered him to his tormentors.

Yes, this parable is about forgiveness, but that forgiveness came out of a willingness of the lord to be patient towards his servant. The kindness that was shown came out of the king's willingness to be *makrothyméō*. That was the request that was made. When we fail to be patient towards all men, we also will be doing a wicked evil thing which could cause someone to suffer, even eternally.

So, when Paul instructs the Church to be *makrothyméō* toward all men, he means that you ought to be yielded to the Spirit of God to the extent that your response to every man in every situation stems from the power of the Spirit which is love displayed in patience motivated by kindness. When you do that, and you are consistently led by the Spirit, there is no opportunity for your old unsaved nature to come out.

This is the same message that Apostle Paul was echoing in his letter to the Corinthian church where he says:

2 Corinthians 5:16
Wherefore henceforth know we no man after the flesh: yea, though we have known Christ after the flesh, yet now henceforth know we Him no more.

When you know no man after the flesh, you base your response to others on who you are in Christ and who you know them to be. Many times you cannot tell the difference between the behaviour of a Christian and that of a non-christian. You will be shocked to find out that the guy who was cursing and swearing at you for pulling off too slowly at the traffic light is actually the head usher at church. He casts off all restraint and behaves just like the heathen who don't know the Holy Spirit. This kind of behaviour quenches the Holy Spirit in your life and hinders His work through you. And He needs to be able to work through you at anytime, anywhere, to reach anybody.

Have you ever woken up one day excited about your faith and asked God to use you mightily to touch somebody's life that day? You go out to face the day with a spring in your step, marching in faith like a good Christian soldier. In your heart, you promise God that you will do whatever He says. Then you sit next to some rough looking fella on the train; I mean tattoos and body piercings everywhere, reeking of beer, and a cigarette hanging out of the corner of his mouth. Then the Lord says, "Let's preach the Gospel to that one." Right there a problem arises. This is the point where many cower away and try to weasel their way out of the promise they made to God earlier in the day.

This is an example of how insensitive Christians can be when they are only seeing through the eyes of flesh. Maybe that fella you are looking at, as rough as he appears, had prayed his last prayer to say, *Lord, if you are real let someone confirm this Gospel I have heard about you*. But because you are not *makrothyméō* towards all men, that soul could be lost forever.

Releasing the Fragrance of Love

As the Holy Spirit began to give me a greater revelation about this instruction to be patient towards all men, I asked Him why this was so important to Him. In answer, He reminded me of a certain woman who had been having problems in her marriage, and she was tired of it. When a woman reaches a point where she says she's tired of her husband, she is tired, and I mean fed up to the back teeth! This woman and her husband were still living in the same place, but they were not together in any sense of the word. They stayed in different parts of the house, and even though they went to the same church, they sat on different sides of the building. They barely spoke to each other, and she especially avoided eye contact with him.

Granted, this woman had gone through a lot to reach this point. She no longer saw any hope or future for them as husband and wife. Had it not been for their children, she would have divorced him. She had forgiven him, but she had been deeply wounded. She made this known to one of the pastors who encouraged her to be patient towards her husband. Instead of divorcing him, she spent more and more time with the Holy Spirit talking with Him and pouring out her heart to Him until her soul was healed. Even though she was no longer in pain, she still had no interest in staying with her husband. In her mind, it was over a long time ago. But then the Holy Spirit gave her one simple instruction, "Show him kindness." And that's what she did.

She started greeting him, giving him eye contact again, and even smiling at him. She still had no feelings towards him, but she did it anyway. She cooked his favourite meals, washed and ironed his clothes again. She even went as far as polishing his shoes and washing his car. Any other act of kindness she could think of, she did it. Before she knew it, her heart was renewed towards him and he too changed his ways. They will soon be celebrating their 20th wedding anniversary. In her pain and anger, she was ready to let her marriage go up in smoke. But because of her willingness to maintain fellowship with the Holy Spirit by being *makrothyméō* towards her husband, He was able to work through that to the salvation of her marriage.

Hello Holy Spirit

It's all about walking in love with the Spirit of God. The Bible says,

1 Corinthians 13:4
Charity [love] suffers long [*makrothyméō*], and is kind...

Let me just add one point of clarification here that to be longsuffering does not mean to suffer long. Patience is the virtue that is required. A commitment to being patient towards all men stimulates kindness, and kindness motivates patience. This is how these two components of the fruit of the Spirit perfectly complement each other. And it is the Holy Spirit who enables you to do both. This is what the Holy Spirit wants and produces as you walk with Him in love.

The prophet Amos asks the question:

Amos 3:3
Can two walk together, except they be agreed?

If you are going to walk with the Holy Spirit and fellowship with Him, you have to agree to move in the same direction He is moving in, and His direction is always love. There's an expression which says, "fight fire with fire" which means you use the same tactics as someone who is opposing you to defeat them. When you do this as a christian, nobody wins, and your wick will burn out quickly. Your fire will quench the Holy Spirit's fire. But when you choose to be patient towards all men, you will be ignited by the Holy Ghost and release the fragrance of His love.

CHAPTER NINE

Render No Evil to Anyone

Mahatma Gandhi once said, "An eye for an eye only ends up making the whole world blind." Prophet Martin Luther King, Jr. picked up the phrase and added, "The time is always right to do the right thing." Unfortunately, many have not adhered to this philosophy. We live in a world where retaliation has become the norm, both physical and verbal. Even the Church has fallen prey to the litigious mindset. It has gotten to the point where protocol has to be established to avoid frivolous lawsuits from petty and spiteful people who call themselves Christians.

We have not only repaid evil, at times we have been the ones to render it. It is foolishness on a rampage! The Bible calls it rendering "evil for evil" which gives us two sides for concern: the evil that is done or perceived as evil, and the evil which is returned in kind. Either way, it is a pervasive infestation that eats away at the unity amongst Christians. But there is a remedy. It's called the fear of the Lord. And I will show you how the fear of the Lord is integral to that component of the fruit of the Spirit we call goodness.

Many have not recognised that the fear of the Lord is one of the secrets to intimacy with the Holy Spirit. The Bible tells us:

Psalm 25:14
The secret of the Lord is with them that fear Him; and He will shew them His covenant.

When we see the word 'secret,' we immediately think of privileged and confidential information that is shared between those who have a close relationship of trust. And it is that. But if you look into that word in its Hebrew form, it is the word *sod*, and one of its meanings is 'friendship.'

The fear of the Lord is a prerequisite for friendship with the Holy Spirit. Furthermore, He is the only member of the Godhead of whom it is expressly stated desires to have an intimate friendship with us. In an earlier chapter, we talked about fellowshipping with the Holy Spirit, and we examined the final verse in 2 Corinthians which says:

2 Corinthians 13:14
The grace of the Lord Jesus Christ, and the love of God, and the communion of the Holy Spirit be with you all.

The "communion" *koinonia* of the Holy Spirit speaks of friendship. The Message translation gets it right which says it like this:

2 Corinthians 13:14 MSG
The amazing grace of the Master, Jesus Christ, the extravagant love of God, the *intimate friendship* [emphasis added] of the Holy Spirit, be with all of you.

Friendship is a both a term and a relationship that is loosely used by many people. Some think everyone is their friend. They, in turn, believe they can be friends with everybody. Some people call those they have just met and know nothing about friends. That's nonsense! How can you be friends with someone you know nothing about? Friendship is built on trust, and trust is based on what you know of the spirit and character of a person. True friendship is a rare and precious thing and should be highly valued and cherished. What is amazing is that the Holy Spirit desires intimate friendship with each of us! We already know that being omniscient God, He knows everything about us; that side of the friendship equation is covered. But if we want to have an intimate *koinōnía* friendship with Him, there are things we need to know and understand about Him too.

Attributes of the Holy Spirit

There is a passage in the Old Testament where the prophet Isaiah shares a few things about the Holy Spirit. Watch what the Bible says:

Isaiah 11:1-3a
And there shall come forth a rod out of the stem of Jesse, and a Branch shall grow out of his roots: 2 and the Spirit of the Lord shall rest upon him, the Spirit of wisdom and understanding, the Spirit of counsel and might, the Spirit of knowledge and of the fear of the Lord; 3 and shall make him of quick understanding in the fear of the Lord.

There are seven attributes of the Holy Spirit and His functions that are given to us in these verses. He is first and foremost, the Spirit of the Lord. He is also the Spirit of wisdom, the Spirit of understanding, the Spirit of counsel, the Spirit of might, the Spirit of knowledge, and the Spirit of the fear of the Lord. For what we are talking about right now, this latter attribute will be our focus: *the Spirit of the fear of the Lord*.

Automatically, when most people hear the word fear, it gives the sense of that which causes us to be fearful or afraid. But that is not what is being communicated right there. Let me remind you of what Paul said to Timothy:

2 Timothy 1:7
God hath not given us the spirit of fear; but of power, and of love, and of a sound mind.

The Spirit of God is not the spirit of fear. Some people hear the title 'Holy Ghost,' and it's like they think He runs around hiding behind corners ready to jump out and shout, "Boo!" No, He doesn't do that. He doesn't promote the kind of fear that the enemy tries to bring into our lives. But (and this is a big but) He is the Spirit who instils in us the fear of the Lord. What then is the fear of the Lord and why is it important and what does it have to do with not rendering evil for evil? Keep reading, and you'll find out.

In the previous chapter, I mentioned something that the prophet Amos said:

Amos 3:3
Can two walk together, except they be agreed?

And I want to reemphasize the necessity for agreement in a relationship with the Holy Spirit with the simple analogy of a three-legged race.

Have you ever seen a three-legged race? It is one of the funniest things to watch. It's a race in which people are put together in pairs. The left leg of one person and the right leg of another is tied together so that they share a leg (so to speak). Then they race against others who are also tied in the same way. There is no way a pair can make any real progress if one tries to move in a different direction than the other. They must move together in the same direction at the same time. This is what Prophet Amos is talking about. To walk with the Holy Spirit, we must move in the same direction He is moving in. His is the dominant "leg" which takes the lead and must be followed.

The Holy Spirit is always moving in the direction of love. At the same time, it's essential for us to remember that He is holy and directly opposed to evil. He is so holy that His eyes are too pure to even look at evil. The prophet Habakkuk declares:

Habakkuk 1:13
Thou art of purer eyes than to behold evil, and canst not look on iniquity...

The Bible is filled with all kinds of language from poetic to prophetic to dramatic and just about everything in between. But very rarely will you find such extreme and strong language as you do when it comes to God's feeling towards and response to evil. There are things God will expressly say that He hates. But there are a few things which He opposes vehemently and communicates that in terms that let us know just how strongly He feels about it. Watch what the Bible says concerning evil:

Romans 12:9
Let love be without dissimulation [*hypocrisy*]. Abhor that which is evil; cleave to that which is good.

Notice, we are not being told to hate that which is evil. No, it's much stronger than that. We are told to *abhor* evil. Abhor is what hate becomes when it graduates. It's another level of hatred. When you abhor something, it means you utterly detest it; you can't stand the sight, smell, taste, or even thought of it. The thing which you abhor becomes an abomination to you, to the extent that the very thought of that thing horrifies you (not in the sense that you are afraid of it, but in the sense that you stay away from it). If we are going to have an intimate friendship with the Holy Spirit, this is what our attitude is supposed to be towards anything evil. It stands to reason then that if we hate evil to that degree, we could not at the same time be rendering it.

Many don't understand why we are so forceful when dealing with anything involving evil or spiritual warfare and such. This is why.

Hello Holy Spirit

You can't cast out the devil while holding his hand at the same time. There are two diametrically opposing sides: good and evil. We are on God's side which is on the side of good. Therefore, when Apostle Paul tells us to "abhor that which is evil," he means hate, despise, detest, recoil, loathe, run for dear life from, turn in horror away from it.

I had to tell you something about evil and God's attitude towards it so that you could better understand the fear of the Lord. In a nutshell, the fear of the Lord means to hate what God hates and to love what God loves. Hate what God says is evil, love what God says is good. That's it! There is no black and white in the issue of good and evil. When you love good, you will automatically hate evil and vice versa because one is opposed to the other.

Proverbs 8:13
The fear of the Lord is to hate evil: pride, and arrogancy, and the evil way, and the froward mouth, do I hate.

The fear of the Lord in both the Old and New Testaments is not a suggestion for the Christian. It is an instruction in righteousness which is necessary for us to follow to avoid grieving the Holy Spirit. It is one of the ways we express our love for Him. Look at what the Bible says in the Old Testament:

Psalm 97:10
Ye that love the Lord, hate evil: He preserveth the souls of His saints; He delivereth them out of the hand of the wicked.

If you love the Lord, hate evil. It doesn't get any plainer than that. And God is gracious: He never gives an instruction He does not empower you to fulfil. The Bible says:

Philippians 2:13
For it is God which worketh in you both to will and to do of his good pleasure.

Not only does God work in you to help you to do what pleases Him, But He also gives you the desire to want to do it. That's how amazing He is! And how does He do this? He does it through the Holy Spirit. The Spirit of the fear of the Lord (who is the Holy Spirit) was with Jesus who is the rod of the stem of Jesse and the Branch spoken of in Isaiah 11:1. Just as the Holy Spirit filled Jesus with the understanding of the fear of the Lord, that same Spirit will to do the same for you and every Christian. All you have to do is ask.

Benefits of the Fear of the Lord

The fear of the Lord ushers you into intimacy with the Holy Spirit to the extent that He can trust you enough to share secrets with you. And as a bonus, there are additional benefits that come along with the fear of the Lord.

There is *preservation* and *deliverance*:

Psalm 97:10
Ye that love the Lord, hate evil: He preserveth the souls of His saints; He delivereth them out of the hand of the wicked.

There is *no lack*:

Psalm 34:9
O fear the Lord, ye his saints: for there is no want to them that fear him.

There is *riches, honour, and life*:

Proverbs 22:4
By humility and the fear of the Lord are riches, and honour, and life.

Hello Holy Spirit

There is *life* and *evil will not find your address*:

Proverbs 19:23
The fear of the Lord tendeth to life: and he that hath it shall abide satisfied; he shall not be visited with evil.

There is *confidence* and *protection for your children*:

Proverbs 14:26
In the fear of the Lord is strong confidence: and his children shall have a place of refuge.

There is a *fountain of life* and *preservation from death*:

Proverbs 14:27
The fear of the Lord is a fountain of life, to depart from the snares of death.

There is *knowledge*:

Proverbs 1:7
The fear of the Lord is the beginning of knowledge: but fools despise wisdom and instruction.

There is *wisdom*:

Proverbs 15:33
The fear of the Lord is the instruction of wisdom; and before honour is humility.

There is *long (or prolonged) life*:

Proverbs 10:27
The fear of the Lord prolongeth days: but the years of the wicked shall be shortened.

There is *special grace* (the secret to Christ's anointing):

Psalm 45:7
Thou lovest righteousness, and hatest wickedness: therefore God, thy God, hath anointed thee with the oil of gladness above thy fellows.

Hebrews 1:9
Thou hast loved righteousness, and hated iniquity; therefore God, even Thy God, hath anointed Thee with the oil of gladness above Thy fellows.

The fear of the Lord brings *rest, edification, and growth*:

Acts 9:31
Then had the churches rest throughout all Judaea and Galilee and Samaria, and were edified; and walking in the fear of the Lord, and in the comfort of the Holy Ghost, were multiplied.

All of these benefits and more are yours as you walk with the Spirit in the fear of the Lord.

Respond with Goodness

Therefore, it is the Holy Spirit who empowers us to carry out the instruction in 1 Thessalonians 5:15. Let's look at it one more time:

1 Thessalonians 5:15
See that none render evil for evil unto any man; but ever follow that which is good, both among yourselves, and to all men.

As we walk with the Holy Spirit, who is the Spirit of the fear of the Lord, we will not render evil to anyone. When evil is done to us, we respond with goodness.

You see, the instruction Apostle Paul gives us in Romans 12:9 is three-fold. Watch what it says:

Romans 12:9
Let love be without dissimulation. Abhor that which is evil; cleave to that which is good.

The prerequisite for all of this is love. If you are not walking in love, you are not walking in the Spirit. You must first of all walk in love by yielding your mind and consequently your actions to the Spirit of God. Allow Him to influence your thoughts, perspective, words, and actions. As you abhor evil and cleave to what is good, you will avoid grieving and quenching Him. We don't have to conform to this world and be spiteful or vengeful. When you find something that God says is good, stick to it like glue!

I don't want you to miss the strength of that word 'cleave' right there. I already implied that it means to stick like glue. When you see that word 'cleave,' picture two pieces of wood stuck together with industrial strength glue. Once they're stuck together, the bond is so great that if you try to pull the two pieces of wood apart, one piece will tear wood away from the other. In cleaving they become fused together, you see. What Paul is saying is, be so stuck on the good that even when someone tries to pull you into evil, they'll be pulling the good right along with you, and that good will overcome their evil.

The instruction in 1 Thessalonians 5:15 is echoed in Paul's instruction to the church at Rome, when he says:

Romans 12:17-21
7 Recompense to no man evil for evil. Provide things honest in the sight of all men. 18 If it be possible, as much as lieth in you, live peaceably with all men. 19 Dearly beloved, avenge not

yourselves, but rather give place unto wrath: for it is written, Vengeance is mine; I will repay, saith the Lord. 20 Therefore if thine enemy hunger, feed him; if he thirst, give him drink: for in so doing thou shalt heap coals of fire on his head. 21 Be not overcome of evil, but overcome evil with good.

You'll never have to worry about taking vengeance or repaying any evil that is done to you. God, who is already opposed to evil, will take care of that better than you ever could.

Most people are familiar with the Nike shoe brand and the accompanying swoosh logo. The name comes from the Greek word *niké* which means 'victory.' This is the root of the word *nikaó* which is translated 'overcome' in this verse. It means that you are victorious over, conquer, and subdue evil when you do good. Good trumps evil every time. It overcomes it just like light overcomes darkness. So, when it comes to doing good, follow the Nike motto and "just do it!"

CHAPTER TEN

Rejoice Evermore

Do you know the shortest verse in the Bible? I know most people think it is "Jesus wept," but not in the original Greek rendering. John 11:35 gives us 'Jesus wept' which has nine letters in English, but in the original Greek rendering, it is *edakrusen o Ihsouv* which is sixteen letters. Yet there is a shorter scripture in the original scripture rendering:

1 Thessalonians 5:16
Rejoice evermore.

Even though it has fifteen letters in English, this is the shortest verse in the Bible, not 'Jesus wept.' In the original Greek rendering, "rejoice evermore" is *pantote cairete* which is fourteen letters. Do you see that? That means it should take you less time to be in rejoicing mode than to weep. You should be instant in joy, that effervescent component of the fruit of the Spirit that we need to rejoice evermore. Rejoicing is more powerful than weeping.

Rejoicing versus Happiness

What does it mean to rejoice evermore? To rejoice means 'to give joy,' 'to feel joy,' and evermore means 'always' or 'forever.' That means rejoicing is a permanent function. It is not dependent on events or happenings. What depends on happenings is happiness, which is a temporary function dependent on events or happenings in the external world. But rejoicing is a derivative of joy, an expression of joy. It is not dependent on what is happening in your external environment. It is from within. It doesn't matter the situation when you have joy in your heart; it is there permanently within your spirit.

Happiness is a state of well-being derived from a happening, but rejoicing is an emotion evoked and expressed by well-being. Do you see the difference? With happiness, you have a state of well-being because of an event that has happened. For example, you get a new suit and when you look at yourself in the mirror you glow and are happy because you look superb in your suit. Rejoicing, on the other hand, is the expression of that well-being that is already inside you. No matter what happens, you have joy and rejoice.

When bad things happen—a summons is in your mailbox, you get fired from your job, you feel sick—those things don't steal your joy because your joy is within, it is inside you, it has permanent residence in you. Because your well-being is not founded on the state of your environment and is rooted deep in your spirit, even when such things happen, you have the audacity to delight.

Rejoicing is not temporary. Notice it says, "evermore." It is permanent. It is forever. It is always with you because it is from within. To rejoice evermore means you believe and have faith in God, that He is doing glorious things in and through all your circumstances because He is able. He can turn evil into good, your mess into a message, and a test into a testimony. Therefore, with joy, it ceases to be about external factors and becomes about the internal. There is a shift from external things being at the centre to the focal point being about what's inside. The question is, how do you get that inner well-being which is permanent? Let's find out.

The Source of Joy

The Bible says:

Galatians 5:22-23
But the fruit of the Spirit is love, joy, peace, longsuffering, gentleness, goodness, faith, meekness, temperance: against such there is no law.

Do you see how you can get the permanent residence of well-being in your spirit? It comes back again to "Hello, Holy Spirit." Without the Holy Spirit you can't get joy, and if you don't have joy, then you can't rejoice because rejoicing is the expression of joy. Remember, you can't give what you don't have. You need joy for you to rejoice, and you need the Holy Spirit for you to have joy because joy is a fruit of the Spirit. Fruit is a result of the tree.

As aforementioned, the Bible doesn't say, the 'fruits' of the spirit; it says the 'fruit' which is singular, and that fruit is one. That fruit is love, so the other facets are part of the singular fruit of love. Do you see that? It's like the Holy Spirit is the tree which has branches, but there is only one fruit. Again for the purpose of illustration, let assume it's an orange. The orange is the fruit, but once you peel the orange, you see different parts of the fruit. Our orange here, which is love, is made up of parts which you can detach as you eat: joy, peace, longsuffering, gentleness, goodness, faith, meekness, and temperance.

Before you have the Holy Spirit, you can't love, and therefore, you can't bear joy. The Holy Spirit is the one who deposits love and joy into your spirit. Watch what the scripture says:

Romans 5:5
And hope maketh not ashamed; because the love of God is shed abroad in our hearts by the Holy Ghost which is given to us.

Do you see what the Holy Spirit does to you? He actually deposits love in your heart, and with this love comes joy and the other parts of love. Do you see now how joy is an internal state of well-being? It is right inside your heart and has nothing to do with what's happening outside your inner world. Rejoicing then is true contentment that comes from the love we have. True joy is everlasting and not dependent on circumstances. Let's take a look at Apostle Paul to get a better insight on joy.

Joy in Bonds

James 1:2-3
My brethren, count it all joy when ye fall into divers temptations; knowing this, that the trying of your faith worketh patience.

Apostle Paul is telling us that even in the midst of temptations and trials, we must never allow such elements to steal our joy. Joy is not variant to these elements. It is independent because our joy is a product of the Holy Spirit and not a product of events or happenings which are external. Apostle Paul is saying we should have joy and we should express it when different temptations come our way, because our faith is being exercised and stretched as temptations are thrown at us, and that's how our faith grows.

Notice faith is like a muscle. It starts small, but as we eat and exercise, the muscle gets nutrition and gets bigger. When you pump weights at the gym, flesh breaks and as it breaks, the body tries to mend the broken parts by creating more flesh. That's how a bodybuilder ends up with big muscles. That is why there is the word 'patience' in our text in James, which in the Greek rendering is *hupomoné*: inner strength which comes from trials, persecutions, and tests. When you experience such things, that is not the time to crumble. Instead, it is the time to express your joy knowing such trials are good for your faith. They give you inner strength and move your faith to its epic level of the God-kind of faith.

Apostle Paul uses the words 'joy,' 'rejoice,' and 'joyful' sixteen times and teaches us how to have true joy despite our circumstances. What gives him the audacity to say count it all joy when we face trials and temptations? Apostle Paul wrote the book of Philippians while in prison in Rome. He was in chains and was aware his life was coming to an end, but he spoke about his faith and trust in Christ. He was imprisoned for two years yet was able to pen over ten letters, even saying, "you are partakers of my grace." Do you see that imprisonment didn't steal his joy? He was in prison, yet he was rejoicing and teaching others about joy. That means, even though his flesh was in prison, his spirit was free and still able to look ahead into the future of others. That's joy! That's rejoicing! The joy inside him wasn't imprisoned. He expressed it through letters which are still giving people joy and comfort today, 2000 years after being penned.

Apostle Paul goes on to say that while he was in prison, the entire Roman guard heard the Gospel from him, and it had even spread throughout all of Rome. Notice what the Bible says:

Philippians 1:18
What then? Notwithstanding, every way, whether in pretence, or in truth, Christ is preached; and I therein do rejoice, yea, and will rejoice.

In and out of prison, he was accomplishing his mission. In and out of prison, he was preaching Christ. And he derived joy because even as he was in prison, his mission was not in prison, his passion for the Gospel was not in prison, and this gave him reason to express his joy. He says, "I therein do rejoice, yea, and will rejoice" in prison. Remarkable! As if that was not enough, he goes on to encourage others to have peace knowing that God strengthens us and supplies our needs according to His riches in glory in Christ Jesus. Do you realise he was pronouncing blessings on those who were outside of prison while he was yet in prison? This is the expression of joy and the pinnacle of rejoicing.

Now I want you to see something else that is extraordinary. Look at this:

Acts 13:52
And the disciples were filled with joy, and with the Holy Ghost.

Notice here that scripture is not telling us that the disciples were filled with joy and then filled with the Holy Ghost. It actually serves to show you the connection between the two and how you cannot have one without the other. The Greek word translated as 'and' in that passage of scripture is *kai* which can be translated as 'even,' 'also,' 'indeed,' or 'and.' In other words, we could have read that scripture as: "**And the disciples were filled with joy, indeed with the Holy Ghost.**" That is why the word is different from the one used for 'and' at the beginning of that verse. That 'and' is *dé* in Greek and it means 'but,' 'moreover,' or just 'and' as it says in that passage.

Paul put a lot of emphasis on this subject, and I could tell how important it was to the Holy Spirit as He took me through all these passages highlighting how Christians can completely stifle Him when they don't yield to this joy that He brings.

Like many of you reading this right now I thought to myself, *I am definitely not one of those who pours water on the Spirit of God like that*. But as He sat there across from me, it was as if He knew what I would think before the thought even entered my mind. He asked me one simple question to make His point.

"Have you ever had something happen to you that upset you so much, and after a while, because you have actually forgotten why you were upset, that joy returns to you?"

Immediately I could recall different scenarios where I had found myself in that kind of situation. So, of course, my answer was yes. But His next question was one that caught me off guard.

"Do you remember how you actually make the effort to recall the thing that upset you, and when you do, you go right back to being as upset as you were when you got the news?"

Then He said,

"That is exactly how you choke and stifle Me: by choosing to go back to the same thing that steals the joy I am trying to bring to you. When you do this, you short-circuit the power of God that should deliver you and change your circumstance."

I knew I had a lot to learn on this subject, so I listened attentively as He began to explain the power of joy. What I learned, and what I'm about to share with you, will blow your mind. Now, let's go back to the book of Acts.

Joy Breaks Prison Gates

The Bible says:

Acts 13:52
And the disciples were filled with joy, and with the Holy Ghost.

Take note of the fact that they were filled with joy and with the Holy Ghost. They came in together because rejoicing and the Holy Spirit are inseparable. For you to be able to express joy, you need the Holy Spirit because the Holy Spirit is the tree which produces the fruit. Joy can't be bottled up inside you. It has to sprout out like fruit springing forth from the branches. It has to come out as rejoicing and be spread around. However, for it to spread, it means you have to be filled. You can't spread what you don't have. You can give off what you have in a small measure, but you have to be filled for you to spread it.

Have you noticed that when people who carry an aura of joy arrive at a place the place lights up with joy? All of a sudden, even if the environment was sombre, joy is spread around the place. That's because joy is contagious. It can rub off on others. Within a fruit there are also seeds to spread and replicate that fruit elsewhere. It's the same with joy. Remember, it's part of the fruit of love which stems from the Holy Spirit. Moreover, this fruit has seeds which have to be spread around so that love and joy can rub off on others. Let me show you an example of what I'm talking about.

There was a time when Paul and Silas were beaten up and stripes laid upon them before being cast into prison. Then the Bible tells us:

Acts 16:24-25
Who having received such a charge, thrust them into the inner prison, and made their feet fast in the stocks. And at midnight Paul and Silas prayed, and sang praises unto God: and the prisoners heard them.

Do you see what the Holy Spirit does? He fills you with joy unspeakable! The disciples, full of joy and the Holy Spirit, were beaten up and thrown into prison. But this was not just a regular part of the prison: it was the inner prison, the part of the prison reserved for hardcore criminals who required maximum security which explains why their feet were also chained. However, notice the beatings and feet stocks couldn't dampen their spirits, it couldn't steal their joy, it was not the end of the world for them. Instead, they searched deep within their spirits and searched for what was not beaten and imprisoned. Their joy was lit and prompted them to pray and sing praises unto God.

Have you noticed when something good happens, people feel like dancing and singing, but when something bad happens they take to complaining, crying, and lamenting? Not Paul and Silas. They had joy, and they had the Holy Spirit inside them. Though their fleshly bodies had been beaten and chained, their joy was free, and they rejoiced so much that the other prisoners heard them. This was not just a song of one who has been forced to sing or was singing for the sake of singing. They sang because they couldn't contain their joy. They were in the inner maximum security prison, but all the other prisoners heard them shouting for joy. Do you see what joy does? You can't contain it even though the facts on the ground don't give you a reason to be happy. Remember, you are not driven by happenings but by what's happening in your spirit.

Now watch what happens next:

Acts 16:26
And suddenly there was a great earthquake, so that the foundations of the prison were shaken: and immediately all the doors were opened, and every one's bands were loosed.

Happiness is dependent on external happenings. Joy, on the other hand, is from within but affects the external environment. Their rejoicing caused the physical realm to shake; it caused the foundations of the prison to shake. Notice happiness shakes you because of what's happening outside, but rejoicing shakes the outside world because of what's happening inside. It's an aura that moves mountains, a force that breaks closed doors, a phenomenon that breaks bands on hands and stocks on feet. Their rejoicing broke the prison gates and set them free.

Do you see the power of joy? Do you see the influence of rejoicing and the power of the Holy Ghost? You cease to be a prisoner of the environment. Instead, the environment bows before you. So, don't allow events to dampen your spirit. Don't allow mishaps to steal your joy. Instead, rejoice evermore and spread the joy around for you are the embodiment of joy. The Holy Spirit gives you this joy which gives you inner peace. It gives you the liberty to say hello freedom, hello peace, hello good life. It makes you feel like rejoicing and shouting, *Hello Holy Spirit*!

CHAPTER ELEVEN

Pray Without Ceasing

When the Holy Spirit gave me this scripture in 1 Thessalonians 5:17 as part of what needed to be done in not quenching Him that afternoon in my house, I found it a very confusing command at first. Does it require us to be like John Fletcher who stained the walls of his room with the breath from his mouth in prayer? Is it saying we should be like the great mystics who have been known to be in trances for years? To pray "without ceasing," according to the verse, seems to imply that we keep praying non-stop. That would suggest a more rigorous regimen than those who I just mentioned. But if that is the case, is praying without ceasing even attainable? I asked the Lord to expound more because to me, that was a very confusing instruction.

Understanding the Scripture

Charles Haddon Spurgeon asked the question, "What do these words imply? 'Pray without ceasing.' Do they not imply that the use of the voice is not an essential element in prayer?" He continues, "It would be most unseemly, even if it were possible, for us to continue unceasingly to pray aloud; there would, of course, be no opportunity for preaching and hearing—for the exchange of friendly conversation, for business, or for any other of the duties of life." With this understanding, the question remains, what then does it mean to pray without ceasing?

It is important for us to understand this part if we are to avoid quenching the Spirit of God. So, I will share with you what He revealed to me as He proved it through the Word of God which He breathed upon that afternoon in October. The question to be answered is, how can we pray without ceasing when we have other things to do in our lives that might take away our time from prayer? Spurgeon's question is then validated because there are a lot of things that need to be done other than prayer. Yet the Bible strictly says:

1 Thessalonians 5:17
Pray without ceasing.

In reality, this scripture is saying: "**Pray continuously without stopping**." The only way you can pray without ceasing is if your praying is fuelled by the particular component of love called faith. But knowing that faith is what is required to carry out this instruction still presents us with a problem. Praying continuously without stopping is difficult to comprehend because it would seem as if we never stop praying. We would have a problem on our hands because we would not be able to do all the other areas that the Holy Spirit in this book says are part and parcel of not quenching the Spirit. I asked the Holy Spirit about this discrepancy because I couldn't figure out how I could accomplish the other aspects of not quenching the Holy Spirit and still pray continuously without stopping.

Without Ceasing

Paul's command in 1 Thessalonians 5:17 to "pray without ceasing," can indeed be confusing if not properly understood. How can we walk around with our eyes closed and heads bowed talking incessantly to God all day every day? While that thought might appeal to those of a more religious inclination, it's impractical at best. How would you be able to get anything else done? Paul could not possibly be referring to non-stop talking.

Hello Holy Spirit

What he is conveying here is more about your attitude than your actions. There ought to be a consciousness of God's presence and an ever-present willingness to respond to and commune with Him at any moment. **Remember prayer is not a monologue so sometimes you not doing the speaking but he is doing the speaking. It's a state of the spirit rather than just a state of the mind.** On it being a state of the mind does not happen automatically. It requires you to put faith in action. This component of the fruit of the Spirit called faith in Galatians 5:22 is the Greek word *pistis* which means belief, trust, confidence, fidelity or faithfulness. As you move in faith with intention and consistency, this consciousness of God's presence becomes second nature until every waking moment is lived in an awareness that God is with you, and He is actively involved and engaged in your thoughts and actions and that he is speaking back in times you are not opening your mouth to pray.

As the Scripture says, we—not God—bring every thought into captivity (see 2 Corinthians 10:5). In everything we are doing, and in every situation we face, we remind ourselves that God is present and ready to communicate with us and help us. This "pray without ceasing" *sunesis* or mindset is prevalent in Paul's letters. Look at what he says in his letter to the Philippians:

Philippians 4:6
Be careful for nothing; but in everything by prayer and supplication with thanksgiving let your requests be made known unto God.

When you by faith maintain this attitude of awareness of the presence of God, if thoughts of doubt, worry, fear, discouragement, or anger come, you consciously and quickly turn them into prayers and thanksgiving. He starts off by saying, don't worry or become anxious about anything ("be careful for nothing"), but then he says, "in everything…" That suggests that we should adopt this mindset in every circumstance.

Apostle Paul taught the Christians at Colosse to devote themselves to continued prayer, being watchful and thankful (see Colossians 4:2). He also exhorted the Ephesian Christians to see prayer as a weapon to use in fighting spiritual battles:

Ephesians 6:18
Praying always with all prayer and supplication in the Spirit, and watching thereunto with all perseverance and supplication for all saints.

As you go through your day, prayer—communicating with God—should be your first response, not only to fearful situations and anxious thoughts but also in sharing your everyday activities and experiences with Him. As you by faith maintain an awareness of God throughout the day, unceasing prayer becomes continual dependence upon and communion with the Father. But initially, this awareness will require some conscious effort. Let me explain what I mean.

Practicing the Presence

When I first started driving, it seemed anything but natural. I had to think about every little thing I did: putting the key into the ignition, changing the gears, steering the car, even putting on my indicators. If someone was in the car with me, I could not talk to them. I was not singing along to any song on the radio or looking around at anything. I had to keep my mind on my driving. But I noticed after driving for some time and gaining more experience, I no longer had to think about it. Now driving has become as natural as walking and talking.

If I were to get in my car now and think through every little action like at first, it would feel abnormal because driving is like second nature to me now. This is how it is when you begin to maintain an awareness of the presence of God and pray without ceasing. At first, the awareness of His presence will require a conscious effort on your part. But after consciously and consistently shifting your thoughts to His presence, it will become so second nature that no matter what else you are doing, you will be conscious that He is right there, and you will be ready to engage with each other at any time.

Praying without ceasing is the conditioning of our spirits to respond to and communicate with the ever-present presence of God at any time. The Bible says:

Acts 17:28
For in Him we live, and move, and have our being...

We don't have to get into God's presence. We are already there. But being aware of that reality changes the dynamics of how we communicate. For example, if I am with my wife, and she is right next to me, I don't have to pick up my mobile phone and call her if I want to talk to her. I can turn my attention towards her at any time and begin communicating, and she can do the same with me whenever she's ready. We are right there with each other, and we are both aware of it. I may even choose another way to communicate with her since I know she is so near. I may reach out to touch her, or I may turn towards her, or I can be there knowing that she knows I'm ready to listen whenever she is ready to say something. I can communicate with her without saying a word because I am aware that she is right there with me. We may not even be talking, but we are still actively engaged with each other's presence. That is what prayer without ceasing is like once you become aware of God's constant presence with you.

The Necessity of Prayer

You see, when you pray without ceasing, it's more about consciousness, an awareness of your spirit. To pray without ceasing is to be conscious of the presence of God and ready to interact with Him to the point where the absence of that consciousness feels abnormal. To borrow an analogy from Pastor-teacher John MacArthur, prayer should be like breathing for Christians. We breathe without thinking about it. He says,

> You do not have to think to breathe because the atmosphere exerts pressure on your lungs and essentially forces you to breathe. That is why it is more difficult to hold your breath than it is to breathe. Similarly, when we are born into the family of God, we enter into a spiritual atmosphere where God's presence and grace exert pressure, or influence, on our lives. Prayer is the normal response to that pressure. As Christians, we have all entered the divine atmosphere to breathe the air of prayer.[1]

Not only should prayer be as natural as breathing, but it is also just as vital. As John MacArthur suggests in his analogy of prayer and breathing, it would be detrimental for us as Christians to think that we can hold our "spiritual breath" and remain unaffected. According to the Guinness Book of World Records, as of the writing of this book, professional freediver Aleix Segura Vendrell holds the record for holding his breath the longest at 24 minutes 3.45 seconds. This is an extraordinary feat, but even Aleix Segura cannot continually hold his breath and remain functional. Just as you cannot hold your natural breath for long without dire consequences, you cannot hold your "spiritual breath" either.

It's interesting to note that when you hold your breath, it is not the lack of oxygen that causes you to gasp for air, but the building up of carbon dioxide inside which causes the lungs and the diaphragm to spasm. Similarly, when you do not pray, it is like the accumulation of spiritual carbon dioxide inside. It won't be long before you find yourself gasping for air. Prayer is vital to the life of a Christian and fellowship with the Holy Spirit. Unfortunately, many Christians deprive themselves of this divine oxygen for extended periods, thinking brief moments with God are sufficient to allow them to survive. But as MacArthur so brilliantly states, "the fact is that every Christian must be continually in the presence of God, constantly breathing in His truths, to be fully functional."

So, why do some Christians deprive themselves of this divine oxygen of prayer? For some, it is a matter of presumption. Some people confuse human success with divine blessing. Consequently, they think that as long as they can carry their own "oxygen tank" of human effort and physical blessings, they no longer need the pure divine oxygen of prayer. They allow other things, like money and human effort, to take the place of God and rob them of their passion to communicate with Him. But the truth is, just as none of us can survive without the continuous flow of oxygen, no matter how great you become, you cannot survive without continually flowing prayer. Whether you realise it or not, you are more dependent on that divine communication than you are on natural oxygen. Continual prayer flows out of humility and dependence on God.

Charles Haddon Spurgeon said:

> Pray without ceasing." That precept at one stroke overthrows the idea of particular times wherein prayer is more acceptable or more proper than at others. If I am to pray

without ceasing, then every second must be
suitable for prayer, and there is not one
unholy moment in the hour, nor one
unaccepted hour in the day, nor one
unhallowed day in the year. The Lord has not
appointed a certain week for prayer, but all
weeks should be weeks of prayer: neither has
he said that one hour of the day is more
acceptable than another. All time is equally
legitimate for supplication, equally holy,
equally accepted with God, or else we should
not have been told to pray without ceasing. It
is good to have your times of prayer; it is
good to set apart seasons for special
supplication—we have no doubt of that; but
we must never allow this to gender the
superstition that there is a certain holy hour
for prayer in the morning, a specially
acceptable hour for prayer in the evening,
and a sacred time for prayer at certain
seasons of the year.

Then as if to answer the question of whether we need to have set times to pray, He goes on to say:

It is good to have your times of prayer; it is
good to set apart seasons for special
supplication—we have no doubt of that; but
we must never allow this to gender the
superstition that there is a certain holy hour
for prayer in the morning, a specially
acceptable hour for prayer in the evening,
and a sacred time for prayer at certain
seasons of the year. [2]

Our Prayer Partner

You see, when we talk about prayer, we are talking about a subject that is very dear to the Holy Spirit. In fact, the Bible tells us that He helps us in our weakness for we know not what we ought to pray for. Watch what the scripture says:

Romans 8:26
Likewise the Spirit also helpeth our infirmities: for we know not what we should pray for as we ought: but the Spirit Himself maketh intercession for us with groanings which cannot be uttered.

The Holy Spirit is an active participator in your prayer life, and when He instructs you to pray without ceasing, He does not mean you should pray an unceasing prayer. There is deeper meaning conveyed in the original language. You see, the Greek word translated as 'without ceasing' in 1 Thessalonians 5:17 is *adialeiptōs*, to do without omission. In other words, when you pray don't leave out the things you desire; don't omit anything. Come boldly to the throne of grace. This word *adialeiptōs* is used four times in the New Testament. I want you to see another scripture where Paul uses that word so you can get a better understanding of his language.

Romans 1:9
For God is my witness, whom I serve with my spirit in the Gospel of His Son, that without ceasing I make mention of you always in my prayers.

Paul was not telling the Roman church that he prays unending prayers for them but that he does not omit to make mention of them in his prayers. Are you getting it now? So, you can be praying but omitting some things that you ought to give to the Lord in prayer. It may even be just praying for a fellow brother in Christ or family member. Nevertheless, God has made that task even simpler because when you pray in the spirit, the Holy Ghost Himself makes up for that inability to know what you should not omit in prayer as the scripture says.

I will never forget a story about a gentleman in Nigeria who came to my man of God Pastor Chris for help. Pastor Chris asked the fella one question, "Have you prayed about this thing you are telling me about?" He replied, "Pastor, last week I prayed for a job, and God answered. I can't come back again today with this new request. Am I His only son? I'm sure He has other things to deal with."

That brother was doing precisely what the Holy Ghost instructs us not to do. When you don't pray you quench the Holy Spirit. He is more than ready to help secure every promise of God in your life. He is able to do exceeding abundantly above all we could ever ask or think. His resources are inexhaustible! He desires so much for every Christians to not lack any good thing to the extent that He will come Himself and help you to pray. Imagine God helping you to ask Himself to give you the thing you want. You just missed an opportunity to shout hallelujah right there! The Holy Ghost is the best prayer partner you will ever have!

---

[1] MacArthur, John. Alone with God: Rediscovering the Power and Passion of Prayer. David C. Cook, 2011.

[2] Spurgeon, Charles Haddon. "Pray Without Ceasing" Sermon. Metropolitan Tabernacle Pulpit, Vol 18, March 10, 1872.

CHAPTER TWELVE

In Everything Give Thanks

Now, I want to show you how self-control—a component of the fruit of the Spirit—relates to our ability to carry out the instruction to give thanks in everything. In fact, self-control is vital to our understanding of and interaction with the presence of God. I know what I'm saying may not make much sense to you right now, but follow me through this chapter. You will see how it all comes together. Let's start with the presence of God.

Many of you know what omnipresent means. When we speak of the omnipresence of God, it means that His presence is everywhere. But we may not have taken the time to think about what that means. The presence of God is everywhere. The Bible tells us:

Acts 17:28
For in Him we live, and move, and have our being...

There is no place you can go where God is not. David understood this when in the psalm he said:

Psalm 139:7-10
7 Whither shall I go from Thy spirit? Or whither shall I flee from Thy presence? 8 If I ascend up into heaven, Thou art there: if I make my bed in hell, behold, Thou art there. 9 If I take the wings of the morning, and dwell in the uttermost parts of the sea; 10 Even there shall Thy hand lead me, and Thy right hand shall hold me.

No matter where you are, the presence of God is, even in Hell. You might be wondering how it can be Hell if the presence of God is there. Well, what makes Hell hellish is not the absence of God but the presence of God not doing anything about the hell you're in. God is everywhere. This is what I'll refer to as the universal presence of God. Everything that happens—the good and the bad—happens in the presence of God. And everything we do, both good and bad, we do in the presence of God.

The Personal Presence of God

God's presence is everywhere. At the same time, we have scriptures that talk about God visiting a place or a person. This refers to what I call His personal or manifested presence. For example, when God was ready to deliver the children of Israel from Egypt, He told Moses, "I am come down to deliver them" (Exodus 3). In Genesis 21:1, we're told that God visited Sarah and she conceived. Before Sodom & Gomorrah were destroyed, God visited Abraham (Genesis 18).

Now I don't want you to get the wrong idea about the personal presence of God. God the Father sits on His throne. So, when we say that God is everywhere, I don't want you to think that He is getting up from His throne and running here and there. That is not the case. The Father sits on His throne, but He can make His presence known in a particular place to a particular person through His Son, through His Spirit, or through any vessel of His choosing.

When Jesus came to Earth, that was the personal presence of God visiting His people, but they failed to recognise it. That's why Jesus said:

Luke 19:43-44
For the days shall come upon thee, that thine enemies shall cast a trench about thee, and compass thee round, and keep thee in

on every side, and shall lay thee even with the ground, and thy children within thee; and they shall not leave in thee one stone upon another; *because thou knewest not the time of thy visitation* [emphasis added].

You see, God was visiting them in the Person of Jesus, but they did not realise it. On that October afternoon, I had an encounter with the personal presence of God in the Person of the Holy Spirit. The point I want you to be clear on is even though the presence of God is everywhere, there is another aspect or manifestation of His presence which is more personal. And everyone does not have the benefit of enjoying that aspect of His presence.

A Refined Presence

When we talk about intimacy with God, we're referring to His personal presence. Intimacy with God is birthed and nurtured in the personal presence of God. God invites us into intimacy with Him which is fellowship with His personal presence. In the Old Testament, the universal presence of God was in the outer courts of the temple, but the personal presence of God was in the Holy of Holies. Not everyone could enter the personal or manifested presence of God. If you were a priest and you did not enter into His personal presence the correct way you would die, because access to the personal presence of God has its own protocol. It follows a different set of rules than access to His universal presence.

His personal presence is a refined presence. He does not manifest His personal presence just anywhere, and while everybody can be in His universal presence, He does not allow just anybody to enter His personal presence. I want to show you a scripture that helps us to understand the personal presence of God in a unique way. It's found in Deuteronomy. For the sake of clarity, I will use The Living Bible translation. Watch what the Bible says:

Deuteronomy 23:12-14
12 The toilet area shall be outside the camp. 13 Each man must have a spade as part of his equipment; after every bowel movement he must dig a hole with the spade and cover the excrement. 14 The camp must be holy, for the Lord walks among you to protect you and to cause your enemies to fall before you; and the Lord does not want to see anything indecent lest He turn away from you.

This might seem like an unusual scripture to use to talk about the personal presence of God. But if you look at it closely, you'll see that it is about more than just where people could go to the toilet. What we're being shown here is that God doesn't want to "walk among" a place if He finds something there that He doesn't like.

The personal presence of God is a refined presence. And there are certain things He expects from those who will fellowship with His presence. This passage lets us know that there is an environment that we can create that is resisted, even avoided, by the personal presence of God. But more importantly, on the flip side of the coin, there is an environment that we can create that attracts and properly hosts the personal presence of God.

Entering His Personal Presence

As I said before, the universal presence of God is everywhere. You don't really have to do anything to get into it. On the other hand, His personal presence can be entered, and there is a specific protocol for doing that. Look at these two passages of scripture from the Psalms:

Psalm 95:2
Let us come before His presence with thanksgiving...

Psalm 100:4
Enter into his gates with thanksgiving, and into his courts with praise: be thankful unto him, and bless his name.

Thanksgiving is the protocol. Gratitude is the key that unlocks the gate to His personal presence. Can you see that? Even when we're dealing with earthly royalty, we understand that to enter their presence they expect a certain standard of behaviour from us. If you were to meet the Queen of England, you are expected to assume a certain attitude and address her in a particular way because she is the queen. How much more the King of the universe? He also has an expectation and a desire to be correctly approached and addressed. Gratitude ushers you into His presence.

When you think about it, you and I are not much different than He is when it comes to gratitude or ingratitude. I don't enjoy being in the company of ungrateful people. God doesn't either. Do you remember when Jesus was carrying out His earthly ministry and He was approached by ten lepers? You'll find the full account in Luke 17:11-19. To recap, there were ten lepers who met Jesus and cried out to Him for mercy. Jesus responded and told them to go and show themselves to the priests. And the Bible says, "as they went, they were cleansed." Now, here is where it gets even more interesting. Let's pick it up from verse 15:

Luke 17:15-19
15 And one of them, when he saw that he was healed, turned back, and with a loud voice glorified God, 16 And fell down on his face at his feet, giving him thanks: and he was a Samaritan. 17 And Jesus answering said, 'Were there not ten cleansed? But where are the nine? 18 There are not found that returned to give glory to God, save this stranger.' 19 And He said unto him, "Arise, go thy way: thy faith hath made thee whole."

I don't want you to miss this. Out of the ten lepers who were cleansed, only one came back to say thank you. You can see from Jesus' response in verses 17-18 that He was expecting the other nine to come back and say thank you also, but they didn't. But notice what He says to the one who did:

Luke 17:19
And He said unto him, "Arise, go thy way: thy faith hath made thee whole."

The one former leper who returned to say thank you received something the others didn't. Jesus said to him, "your faith has made you whole." That one leper's expression of thanksgiving gave him something that the others did not get because of their ingratitude. Seeing that thankfulness is something the Lord expects and that it can give us something we might not get otherwise, we need to take a closer look at what being 'thankful' means.

Say Thank You

Most standard dictionaries will define the word 'thankful' to mean 'to express gratitude and relief' or 'to show appreciation.' Appreciation is the recognition of goodness. So, when you're thankful, you recognise goodness and express gratitude for it. In 1 Thessalonians 5:18, the word 'thanks' is *eucharistéō* which means to express gratitude towards. Some people refer to the Holy Communion as the Eucharist which means 'the giving of thanks' or 'thanksgiving.' It is impossible to be thankful and keep quiet. Thanksgiving has to be expressed.

One of the things I teach my children is the importance of saying 'Thank you.' This simple expression of gratitude can open doors for you. The opposite is also true: failure to express gratitude can close doors. Anyone to whom you show favour who does not know how to respond constrains you from doing more. This principle also applies to how we relate to the Holy Spirit. A simple thank you is what qualifies you for the next act of favour.

The Danger of Complaining

Most people would say that the opposite of thanksgiving is ingratitude, but the opposite of thanksgiving is complaining. Thanksgiving means to express appreciation for goodness. Complaining, on the other hand, means to find fault and to express dissatisfaction. Throughout the Scripture, you will often see murmuring and complaining mentioned side by side because they go together. Here's another notable parallel between thanksgiving and complaining: you can be ungrateful and not say a word, but complaining, like thanksgiving, is expressed. One is an expressed recognition of goodness. The other is identifying what you see as not good and expressing that, but there is danger in doing that.

There are a couple of passages to which I will refer that will help you understand how God feels about complaining and how He responds to it. I encourage you to go back to and read them in their entirety later on. One of those passages is in Numbers 16:41-50. When you read this passage, you'll see that the people complained against God's leaders, Moses and Aaron, behind their backs. What those people didn't and some Christians today still don't realise is that when you complain about anything, you complain in the presence of God. And as I said earlier, He does not like to be in the presence of people who are complaining. So much so, that in this passage when the people complained, 14,700 of them were killed as a result. Apostle Paul, referring to this account, explains how it happened:

1 Corinthians 10:10
Neither murmur ye, as some of them also murmured, and were destroyed of the destroyer.

Just so there's no misunderstanding about what the word 'murmur' is talking about, let's look at the same verse in the New King James Version:

Nor complain, as some of them also complained, and were destroyed by the destroyer.

The words 'murmur' and 'complain' are used interchangeably. Now I don't want you to miss what happened as a result of their complaining. The scripture says God allowed a destroying angel to kill nearly 15,000 complaining people with a plague. You don't allow such a thing unless you feel very strongly about it. Let's look at another passage that shows us how God feels about complaining.

In Numbers 21:4-10 we have another account of the people complaining. These people were really pushing it this time because it says that the people complained against Moses and God too! Because of their complaining, God allowed venomous snakes to bite them—the Bible calls them fiery serpents—and many of the people died. We don't know how many died, the Bible doesn't mention that; but if God says there were many, there were many! Now in this account in Numbers, the people recognized that it was their complaining that had caused the fiery serpents to bite them. Watch what the Bible says:

Numbers 21:10
Therefore the people came to Moses, and said, "We have sinned, for we have spoken against the Lord, and against thee; pray unto the Lord, that He take away the serpents from us." And Moses prayed for the people.

Remember, these people were in the wilderness. Those snakes were there all along, but God had been protecting the people from them. That brings me to my next point: when you complain, you leave yourself open to the attacks of the enemy. Complaining is one way you can break the hedge of protection, for the Bible says:

Ecclesiastes 10:8
He that diggeth a pit shall fall into it; and *whoso breaketh an hedge, a serpent shall bite him* [emphasis added].

When you are a thanks giver, you are enveloped and cocooned in the protective presence of God. You become unreachable, untouchable. You need to understand that even that which you think is yours here on Earth already belongs to God. The only thing He cannot give to Himself is thanks. That is why He is always around those who praise and thank Him. We have seen from the two passages in Numbers how strongly God feels about complaining, and implicitly, how valuable those who thank Him are to Him. Now let's see why.

Why God Hates Complaining

I asked God why He hates complaining so much, and He gave me two answers in response. The first has to do with His goodness. You see when we complain, we actually side with the enemy against God's goodness. We know that Satan is called and is the accuser of the brethren. But what we don't realise is that when we complain, in effect we become God's accusers. Let me explain.

When God proclaimed His character to Moses (in Exodus 34:5-6), He described Himself as being "abundant in goodness." We often say, "God is good all the time, and all the time God is good!" And it's true. He is always good. But a complaint says to God, You're not good *enough*. For example, Apostle Paul says of God that He will supply all of your need according to His riches in glory by Christ Jesus (Philippians 4:19). That's the goodness of God. But when you turn around and complain about what you don't have, you have in effect raised an accusation against the verity of God's goodness. This is the first reason He hates complaining.

Any statement that opposes or contradicts the goodness of God in your life is a complaint, and a complaint is an attack on the very character of God. Because of that, He takes complaining personally, and there is always a consequence. It might not be as obvious as a physical plague or venomous snakes. But to me, the worst consequence is what He communicated to me in the second part of His answer. When you complain, you are not able to access and enjoy the personal presence of God.

It's not difficult to understand this answer when you look at it in the context of what He has already said about thanksgiving. In the verses we read in the Psalms, we saw that thanksgiving gives us access to His personal presence. If thanksgiving is like a key that allows you to enter the gates of His personal presence, then complaining is like a lock that keeps you from entering. And He doesn't want that. He wants you to have intimacy with Him.

Apostle Paul tell us:

Philippians 2:14
Do all things without murmurings [complaining] and disputings [arguing].

If you compare that verse with our key verse in 1 Thessalonians 5:18, you will see they are parallel in meaning. In other words, if we are going to give thanks in everything, it means that we do all things without complaining.

The Power of Self-Control

We need to remember God has not changed. Even though we're under grace, He's still the same God now as He was back then. That means that He hates complaining as much now as He did back then. As I said in a previous chapter, one of the ways we demonstrate our love for God is to love what He loves. God loves, values, and appreciates when we give Him thanks.

The Holy Spirit wants to fellowship with us, but if we are complaining, it pours cold water on His fire. Complaining is decidedly not a part of the fruit of the Spirit. Moreover, complaining works against the fruit of love and grieves the Holy Spirit. Instead of attracting the presence of the Holy Spirit, complaining causes Him to withdraw and stop speaking. Instead of complaining, we ought to exercise self-control and give thanks.

To show you how this works, let's look one more time at our focus verse:

1 Thessalonians 5:18
In everything give thanks: for this is the will of God in Christ Jesus concerning you.

What I'm about to say is a revelation you cannot afford to miss. The verse says, "in everything give thanks." I know some of you are wondering how you can give thanks in the midst of terrible situations. Let me assure you, God is not telling you to lie about your external circumstances. What He is telling you to do is look inside. That means that no matter how negative a situation looks, don't just look *at* it, look *in* it! If you take the time to look in it, you will find something to be thankful for. Many people wonder what the will of God is for their lives, but you don't have to wonder about this one. He expressly says, "this is the will of God in Christ Jesus for you." This is what He wants you to do: give thanks in everything.

To give thanks in everything, you need the ability to react in a good way even when bad things are happening. That requires self-control. Translated from the Greek word *enkráteia*, self-control is what enables you to dominate the inclination to complain rather than give thanks. You can be looking at an unpleasant situation or circumstance, and the temptation arises to complain about it. But with *enkráteia*, it is as though the hand of your spirit reaches out and pushes you towards giving thanks instead.

Spiritually, complaining leaves a bitter taste in your mouth, but thanksgiving cleanses the palate. If you want to be attractive to the Holy Spirit, be intentional about being thankful. It makes you irresistible to His presence. Don't get caught up in what I call candy-coated complaints. Candy-coated complaints are complaints that don't sound like complaints, but they really are. You say something negative, but then immediately follow-up with something like, "But God is good!" Just leave out everything up to and including the 'but' and only express gratitude for the good parts.

Despite what it looks like in any given situation, before you open your mouth to say something negative, look for God's goodness. Look for it! I promise you will find it. And when you do, thank Him for it. If you make thankfulness your habit and your lifestyle, you will transform your environment and free up the Holy Spirit to work with you and for you. Not only that, the more you give thanks, the more you'll enjoy greater intimacy with the wonderful Holy Spirit!

CHAPTER THIRTEEN

Despise Not Prophesyings

Previously, we saw how walking with the Spirit in love produces the kind of faith that enables us to carry out the instruction to pray without ceasing. Here again, we will see how faith is required to "despise not prophesyings." Prophecy is the response of the prophet's spirit to the audible voice of God. Faith is the positive response of the human spirit to the Word of God. Faith is what gives us the ability to respond to what is important.

My man of God and mentor, Pastor Chris Oyakhilome, taught me an invaluable lesson about the difference between value and importance. I'll use the following illustration to relate the crux of what he said. Let's say my shoes cost £2,000, and my Phone costs £1,000. My shoes are more valuable than my Phone. But on my Phone, I have all of my most important contacts, phone numbers of my mentors, my pastors, and so on. If something happened to my shoes, I would simply replace them. But if I lost or misplaced my Phone, I would do everything I could to get it back; because even though my shoes are more valuable, what is on my Phone is more important.

All people have value. But all people are not the same. All Christians have value, but all Christians are not equally important. We were all bought by the Blood of Jesus. One price: the blood. But don't confuse your value with your importance to God. Some people are more important to God than others, even though the value is the same. You may not be as important to God as Benny Hinn who has won millions to Christ if you've not done the same yourself. Pastor Chris Oyakhilome has hundreds of thousands attending his services every week and is touching countless millions through other media. Do you suppose you are as important to God as he is if you're not doing exactly as he is doing? The Apostle Paul tells us:

Romans 12:3
For I say, through the grace given unto me, to every man that is among you, not to think of himself more highly than he ought to think; but to think soberly, according as God hath dealt to every man the measure of faith.

Apostle Paul is not saying that you should not think highly of yourself. That's not what he's saying at all. You are undoubtedly valuable to God, so valuable that He sent His Son Jesus to die for you. What Paul is saying is that you should not regard yourself "more highly" than you ought to. In other words, think highly of yourself—attribute to yourself the value that God attributes to you. At the same time, recognise there are those who have received grace to rise to levels to which you have not yet attained; those who are making a greater impact for the Kingdom of God than you are.

There was a woman spoken of in Acts 9:36-42 by the name of Tabitha (translated in the Greek as Dorcas). This woman was known because of the good she had done for so many and as a giver. Much to the dismay of all those who loved her, she got sick and died. It happened that Apostle Peter was in the area at the time, so they called him to come. When he arrived, the widows were weeping and showing him all the things Tabitha had made. After Peter put everyone out of the room, through the power of God he raised Tabitha from the dead. If this woman had been just an insignificant person, as valuable as her life was, she would have remained dead and been buried. But because this woman was important and had made a Kingdom impact, the people sent for Peter and she was raised from the dead.

Prophets Are Important

God is a Prophet before anything else, and His utterances are prophetic. In Genesis, the Bible says, "And God said..." He declares beforehand what will be. Prophets are a particular replication of God as Prophet. You see, a prophet is the mouthpiece of God, His biological microphone. When God wants to speak, He only speaks through a prophet or a prophetic utterance. Now I want you to think about that for a moment because if God does not speak, there is nothing for us to say. If He does not say anything, nothing would or will exist. God brings everything into existence with the words of His mouth, and His "mouth" in the Earth are His prophets. They are not just valuable, but they are also important. Watch what the Bible says:

Amos 3:7
Surely the Lord God will do nothing, but He revealeth His secret unto His servants the prophets.

God does nothing unless He reveals it one of His prophets somewhere. Did you get that? God gives exclusive information, secrets of God, that He reveals only to His servants the prophets. They are divinely inspired to declare the purposes of God.

Prophets are not ordinary people. They are extraordinary people who are visited by God. The first thing that happens to a prophet is God visits you and tells you that you are one. For those of you who are wondering whether you're a prophet or not, let me help you. You're not one. Prophets know they are prophets because God makes that known to them and puts them in a distinct and separate category of people. Look at what the Bible says:

Despise not Prophesyings

1 Chronicles 16:20-22
And when they went from nation to nation, and from one kingdom to another people; 21 He suffered no man to do them wrong: yea, he reproved kings for their sakes, 22 Saying, "Touch not mine anointed, and do My prophets no harm."

I want you to notice what God Himself is saying here. He puts His people in two categories: My anointed and My prophets. Of one group of people, His anointed, He says don't touch them. You would think that would have been enough since prophets are among His anointed. But God adds another clear level of distinction by singling out His prophets from the rest of His anointed people, and says, "and do My prophets no harm." If you can't see the distinction of importance there, then you are like a blind man with his eyes closed wearing dark sunglasses at midnight!

Now before we move on, I want to point out something else that God is saying in verse 22. The word there for 'touch not' is the Hebrew word *naga* which means to touch in a harmful way. But that is not the word used for 'no harm' referring to the prophets. That word is the Hebrew word *ra* which means evil or to do wickedly. This differentiation between *naga* and *ra lets* us know that doing evil to a prophet is something other than touching the Lord's anointed in a harmful way. That begs the question, how then is evil done to a prophet? One of the primary ways a person can do evil to a prophet is given in our focus verse for this chapter:

1 Thessalonians 5:20
Despise not prophesyings.

Let us examine this further.

Harming God's Prophets

I remember sitting near a young prophet on one particular occasion. He was both young in age and spiritual maturity. For no apparent reason, he opened his mouth and began to bad-mouth another prophet of God. Interestingly enough, the prophet he was talking about is walking in levels of prophetic grace that this young prophet has only dreamed of reaching. Here is something even more ironic. One of the people this young man greatly respected in the prophetic and longed to be mentored by was the spiritual father of the prophet he was bad-mouthing. He had no idea that by speaking against a prophet of God, he had spoken against himself. Using your words to speak evil of a prophet of God is one way that you can do harm. Another way you can use words to do harm is to despise him by treating what he says with "dismissive disdain."

You see, the strength of a prophet is in his words. He is the mouthpiece of God, and God speaks. So, whenever a prophet of God speaks, it is as if God Himself is speaking even when He hasn't said anything. I want you to see an example of what happened when someone treated the words of the prophet Elisha with dismissive disdain. Let's look at two related passages from 2 Kings in the New King James version:

2 Kings 6:33
And while [Elisha] was still talking with them, there was the messenger, coming down to him; and then the king said, "Surely this calamity is from the Lord; why should I wait for the Lord any longer?"

2 Kings 7:1-2
Then Elisha said, "Hear the word of the Lord. *Thus says the Lord* [emphasis added]: Tomorrow about this time a seah of fine flour shall be sold for a shekel, and two seahs of barley for a shekel,

at the gate of Samaria." So an officer on whose hand the king leaned answered the man of God and said, "Look, if the Lord would make windows in heaven, could this thing be?" *And he* [Elisha] *said* [emphasis added], "In fact, you shall see it with your eyes, but you shall not eat of it."

Notice in 7:1 Elisha says, "Thus says the Lord..." But in the latter part of verse 2 there is no "Thus says the Lord," yet Elisha's words still came to pass just as if God Himself had spoken them. Now let's go back and take a closer look at the officer's response to the prophet's words:

2 Kings 7:2
So an officer on whose hand the king leaned answered the man of God and said, "Look, if the Lord would make windows in heaven, could this thing be?"

The officer treated the words of the prophet with dismissive disdain. He didn't believe the words of the prophet, and he took it a step further by treating the prophet's words contemptuously. He acted like the prophet was to be taken as a fool. What's more, he did it publicly. But watch what happens:

2 Kings 7:17-20
17 Now the king had appointed the officer on whose hand he leaned to have charge of the gate. But the people trampled him in the gate, and he died, just as the man of God had said, who spoke when the king came down to him. 18 So it happened just as the man of God had spoken to the king, saying, "Two seahs of barley for a shekel, and a seah of fine flour for a shekel, shall be sold tomorrow about this time in the gate of Samaria." 19 Then that officer had answered the man of God, and said, "Now look, if the Lord would make windows in heaven, could such a thing be?" And he had said, "In fact, you shall see it with your eyes,

but you shall not eat of it." 20 And so it happened to him, for the people trampled him in the gate, and he died.

The thing that Elisha said would happen according to the Word of the Lord happened just like he said. And the thing he uttered by his own prophetic declaration without the Lord saying anything, also happened. The officer was trampled to death. Just as the prophet declared, he lived long enough to see the famine end, but not long enough to enjoy the blessings of the fulfilled Word of the Lord. It's a dangerous thing to despise the words of a prophet of God.

The Prophetic is for You

When you read the Scripture, you do not see God running around begging people to love Him. Neither do you see Him repeatedly asking people to follow Him. But over and over God expresses His desire for people to believe what He says. The Bible says:

Psalm 138:2
I will worship toward Thy holy temple, and praise Thy name for Thy lovingkindness and for Thy truth: for Thou hast magnified Thy word above all Thy name.

God places supreme importance on His Word even more than His own name. If He puts that much importance on what He says, we can be sure He never talks just for the sake of talking. So, when God speaks through His prophet, He wants you to believe what He says knowing it is for your own blessing and benefit not the prophet's. Here's a funny little story to illustrate my point.

One of my pastors was supposed to be at a specific location but he was running late. Just as I was beginning to wonder what was taking him so long to get there, he called me and said he couldn't find his keys. Immediately, in the realm of the Spirit, I saw exactly where his keys were. I told him they were under a pillow in his room. He went straight to the location and recovered his keys. But after I hung up the phone with him, I couldn't find my own keys. And the same pastor whose keys I had located prophetically had to come by and pick me up for the service.

People may find it hard to believe that after prophesying to millions of people, I cannot use my prophetic grace to find my own lost keys. And if my wife BeBe and I are in the same boat, then we're really in trouble! You see, the prophetic grace of the prophet is for you, not himself or herself. That's why it is important for you to believe the words of a prophet of God. When a prophet prophesies, he has to use faith to declare the Word which he receives. You also need to use your faith to believe and act upon the prophetic word that you hear.

Now the verse in 1 Thessalonians 5:20 says, "despise not prophesyings" or don't despise prophetic utterances. The word 'despise' is translated from the Greek word, *exoutheneó* and it means to despise, 'to make of no account; make contemptible; set at nought so that it doesn't work.' It is as though there is a scale of importance, zero being of no importance and ten being most important. Then when the prophet of God speaks, the one who despises the prophetic utterance says in his or heart, that's a zero. If you despise the prophetic word, you dishonour God, and His Word cannot work for you.

The Most Important Thing

When it comes to the things of God, honour is at the top of the list. Honour is everything! To honour means 'to give weight,' 'to make heavy,' 'to glorify.' It means to give the utmost respect. When we honour God, we give His Word more respect or weight in our lives than anything else. And when a prophet of God speaks, we should give his words the same weight of importance as if God Himself is speaking directly to us; because in fact, He is. All the Apostle Paul is saying is take prophetic utterances seriously.

That presents a problem for most people because they don't recognise a prophetic utterance, so they miss it. A prophet of God does not always speak in 17th century English like the King James Bible. He may not get up and declare, "Thus saith the Lord!" He may just stand in front of the people and say, "Lift your hands." People will often miss something like that as a prophetic utterance and will ignore the instruction not realising that it came directly from the mouth of God.

I remember a story I heard about a boy who was playing in his yard. The boy's father was standing on the porch watching his son play in the dirt. All of a sudden, the father shouted, "Run!" The boy did not stop to question the father or the importance of what he was saying. He just took off running towards his dad. When he got up on the porch with his father, he looked back and saw a snake slithering right near where he had been standing. If the words of that father had been a prophetic instruction, some of you would have been bitten by that snake. Not following simple prophetic instructions can grieve the Holy Spirit because what many don't know is those utterances come from Him.

The Spirit of Prophecy

Prophets speak by the power of the Holy Spirit. What I mean by that is, when I prophesy, it's the Holy Spirit showing me things and telling me what to say. Do you remember Jesus saying that the Holy Spirit will testify of Him? Let's look at it:

John 15:26
But when the Comforter is come, whom I will send unto you from the Father, even the Spirit of truth, which proceedeth from the Father, He shall testify of Me.

Then in another place, the Bible says:

Revelation 19:10
For the testimony of Jesus is the spirit of prophecy.

The Person who gives the testimony of Jesus is the Holy Ghost, the One who Jesus said "shall testify of Me." Can you see now how despising prophecy will grieve the Spirit of God? It is the Holy Spirit who makes the things of God known to us.

The word 'prophecy' is the Greek word *prophéteia*. It is derived from two Greek words: *pró* which means 'before' and *phēmí* which means 'to make clear or assert as a priority.' Prophecy then is communicating and enforcing revealed divine truth that is clarified beforehand. And no one does that better than the Holy Spirit. It is the Holy Spirit who takes God's plans and preparations and reveals them to us. Watch what the Bible says:

1 Corinthians 2:9-11
9 But as it is written, "Eye hath not seen, nor ear heard, neither have entered into the heart of man, the things which God hath prepared for them that love Him." 10 But God hath revealed them unto us by His Spirit: for the Spirit searcheth all things, yea, the deep things of God. 11 For what man knoweth the things of a man, save the spirit of man which is in him? Even so the things of God knoweth no man, but the Spirit of God.

No man knows the things of God except by the Spirit of God. The Bible is a prophetic book filled with the utterances of God and every word was revealed and written under the inspiration of the Holy Spirit. The Bible confirms this when it says:

2 Timothy 3:16
All scripture is given by inspiration of God, and is profitable for doctrine, for reproof, for correction, for instruction in righteousness.

All scripture, not some scripture, is given by inspiration of God. It is God-breathed and the One doing the breathing is the Spirit of God. Watch what the Bible says:

2 Peter 1:20-21
Knowing this first, that no prophecy of the scripture is of any private interpretation. For the prophecy came not in old time by the will of man: but holy men of God spake as they were moved by the Holy Ghost.

It is clear from the scriptures that there would be no declared or written Word of God without the involvement of the Holy Spirit.

The Standard of Persecution

Prophets have always been mistreated by people. Even Jesus acknowledged this when He said:

Matthew 5:11-12
Blessed are ye, when men shall revile you, and persecute you, and shall say all manner of evil against you falsely, for my sake. Rejoice, and be exceeding glad: for great is your reward in heaven: for so persecuted they the prophets which were before you.

It's as if He was saying that prophets are the standard for persecution. But even though some people seek to do them harm, they are exceedingly loved by God. I believe the Holy Spirit most closely identifies with prophets than any others in the Body of Christ. He, like them, is often misunderstood, ignored, and spoken of with evil intent. Like the prophets, people often try to use Him for what He can do rather than getting to know Him for who He is. His Word is not without power, and neither are those of the prophets of God. Therefore, when you hear prophetic utterances, don't despise them. Instead, recognise the importance of the ones carrying it and respond in faith to what you hear so that the blessings which those utterances carry can become your reality.

CHAPTER FOURTEEN

Prove All Things

Gullibility is not an attractive trait for Christians. You should not blindly trust everything you hear just because it's coming from behind a pulpit. What people say God is saying is not always the same as what He is saying. That's why Apostle Paul places the responsibility on every Christians to "prove all things." This mandate is both indicative of our ability to do it and of its necessity.

It is critical for us to develop the habit of proving or testing the things that we hear so that we will not fall into error and deception. This requires patience, a component of the fruit of the Spirit. We have seen how patience works with kindness in being patient with all men. Now I will show you how to use it to "prove all things."

The Bible tells us:

Hebrews 5:14
But strong meat belongeth to them that are of full age, even those who by reason of use have their senses exercised to discern both good and evil.

It takes practice, the exercising of your spiritual senses, to discern what is good and evil. The more you grow in the things of God, the easier it will become to distinguish what you need to keep as coming from God, and what you need to throw out.

I like to eat fish, but because of something that happened to me years ago, I am very careful not to swallow any bones. When I was very young, someone gave me a piece of fish to eat, but I did not know there were bones in the fish. Since I trusted the one who gave it to me, I had no reason to believe that I was in any danger, but I was. I ate it too quickly and a bone got caught in my throat. Every time I tried to swallow, I could feel the bone getting pushed a little deeper scraping the sides of my throat. I was panicking because, though it was only moments, it felt like time stood still and I was sure I was going to choke to death. Somehow the bone got dislodged, and I was able to swallow normally. My life was spared that day from the slow painful death of a fish bone caught in my throat.

A Serious Offence

That story is funny to me now, but it was not funny at the time. It was a serious issue. I learned a valuable lesson that day which I am passing on to you in six simple words: eat the fish, leave the bones. That paraphrases what the Apostle Paul says when he writes:

1 Thessalonians 5:21
Prove all things; hold fast what is good.

This brings balance to what we discussed in the previous chapter. Too many Christians are being handed and hungrily gobbling down what looks like fish, but spiritually speaking, it has a lot of bones in it. Because of immaturity and inexperience, many Christians are choking on the bones of false doctrines, unbiblical teaching, and "prophe-lying" (rather than true prophesying). That is why we must test what we hear.

The test or proof of a thing is only necessary when there is the possibility of counterfeit. We believe the Bible in its entirety to be the inspired Word of God and the infallible rule of faith and conduct. At the same time, we understand that the hearts and mouths of some who communicate that Word are not always pure and inerrant. Consequently, they taint and distort the Word of God, and sometimes just flat out lie and introduce counterfeit into the Church.

Counterfeit is a problem inside and outside of the Church. Right now, of all the currency in circulation at any given time, a small percentage of it is counterfeit. It's an offence to be in possession of counterfeit money without a lawful reason or excuse. If you are found with counterfeit money in your possession in the United Kingdom, you could face a minimum of two years in prison. And if you knowingly keep or try to pass off counterfeit money as real, you'll face up to ten years in prison.

Counterfeiting is a serious offence, and it has an even more detrimental effect when it's found in our churches. Therefore, when you are in a position to communicate the Word of God in any form, whether it be teaching, preaching, prophesying, or whatever form the handling of the Word takes, you must do it with great care and diligence. Failure to do so not only misrepresents God but can also cause those who have not yet learned to discern good and evil to stumble. No wonder the Bible says:

James 3:1
My brethren, let not many of you become teachers, knowing that we shall receive a stricter judgment.

While this places a great responsibility on those who communicate the Word, that does not give any Christian the excuse to neglect their own careful examination of the Word.

Due Diligence

Caveat emptor, a Latin term that means "let the buyer beware," is something I always keep in mind when doing my real estate dealings. When I am interested in purchasing a property, the one selling the property will usually try to make me as a potential buyer or investor aware of all the best features of the property. If there is something wrong with the property, the seller may or may not fully disclose that to me. Therefore, it is in my best interest to exercise due diligence. That means I do a patient and thorough investigation of what is being presented to me before I sign on the dotted line and buy what they're selling. This principle can likewise be applied to what is being "sold" to you from behind a pulpit. Let the "buyer" beware!

Sometimes people blame pastors and other leaders for what they didn't know or were subjected to from behind the pulpit. But the fact of the matter is, we all have access to the Bible. What's more, you have the Holy Spirit. The bottom line is every Christian is responsible for performing due diligence. This is what Paul is referring to when he says you must "prove" all things.

The word 'prove' is replete with meaning. It is translated from the Greek word *dokimazó*, which means, "to test, examine, prove, scrutinize (to see whether a thing be genuine or not), as metals."[1] It comes from the word *dókimos* which describes someone who would not accept or circulate counterfeit money. You see, in ancient times, metal coins were used for currency, and each coin was supposed to have a certain weight. But there were deceitful people who would shave down the coins so that their weight was less than what it was supposed to be. If a money changer was *dókimos*, it meant that he would make sure that only approved, fully weighted genuine money would go into circulation.

So, when Paul instructs us to *dokimazó* all things, he is saying that you must be like the *dókimos* and refuse to accept or put into circulation anything that is counterfeit or unapproved. Also, the present tense of the word tells us that this is to be a continuous action. It is imperative. That means that we must, we are commanded to, "prove all things." However, "all things" in this instance does not mean everything.

Narrow Your Scope

If you tried to test every single thing you heard or read, you would wear yourself out. Take the Internet and the media for example. There is an overwhelming abundance of information coming at you. Unfortunately, there are people who are gullible enough to believe just about anything they read on the Internet or hear about in the media. They don't seek to verify anything. They just take it and run with it. Just because you see it on the Internet or hear about it in the media, does not mean that it's true. There is a lot of false information available. There are agencies even on the Internet that make it their responsibility to verify rumours and other information to see if it's true. They refer to themselves as "fact-checkers." To test or verify everything might sound appealing in concept, but practically, it would be overwhelming.

To be able to carry out the mandate to "prove all things" in the context of what we're talking about, we have to narrow the scope. When Paul says, "all things," he is not referring to an all-encompassing "all." He is referring to those things which are being communicated to you as spiritual truth. That is what must be verified. And one way you can do this is by using a method similar to what the ancient *dókimos* money changers used to detect counterfeit currency.

Check the Weight

In ancient times, the *dókimos* money changers would already know what the approved weight of each coin should be. All they would need to do is compare the suspect coin with a coin that they know is approved. This practice is very similar to modern-day counterfeit banknote detection. The basic premise of counterfeit banknote detection is to become so familiar with a genuine approved banknote that you can easily spot a fake.

Counterfeit detection agents know what the real thing looks, feels, and sounds like. This familiarity with the authentic is what gives them the ability to quickly detect a counterfeit. Your Bible is the real thing. Open it. Read it. Study it. Know what it looks, feels, and sounds like so that when someone tries to pass along something fake, you will already be prepared to detect it.

Verify It

Another way you can "prove all things" is to follow-up on what you hear before you accept it as truth. Many people take notes when they are listening to what they believe to be good Bible teaching or preaching. Some will go back and reread their notes and meditate on what they have heard. And then there are those who will go back and look into those things they have heard to check them out and see if they line up with the Scriptures. Paul encountered a group of people who were known for this. Let's look at what the Bible says:

Acts 17:10-11
And the brethren immediately sent away Paul and Silas by night unto Berea: who coming thither went into the synagogue of the Jews. These were more noble than those in Thessalonica, in that they received the word with all readiness of mind, and searched the scriptures daily, whether those things were so.

If ever a source of information were credible, it would be Paul. Still, he commended the Bereans for checking out the things he said to see "whether those things were so." More than likely he witnessed them doing this, or they came back to him with questions or comments that let him know that they had been searching the scriptures. We also ought to thoroughly examine and test by the scriptures the teachings, doctrines, and prophetic utterances to which we are exposed. Check out what you hear and see if it lines up with the Word. If it doesn't line up, no matter who it came from, throw it out! If you practice doing this, it will keep you from falling prey to deception.

Think About It

Let me just pause right here and expose a common fallacy in the Body of Christ that says you are not supposed to question anything you hear from behind the pulpit. There is nothing unspiritual or unscriptural about asking questions. God is not so insecure that He can't handle you asking questions. God is a Master Teacher, in fact, the Supreme Teacher. And any church leader worth their salt will encourage earnest and sincere questions.

Sceptic turned Christian apologist and evangelist, Ravi Zacharias has a broadcast called, "Let My People Think." Strangely enough, thinking is almost a lost art in Christian circles. People listen to messages, teachings, and other prophetic utterances and just swallow everything thrown in their path like Pac-Man. In actuality, we should be among the best thinkers in the world because of what we have. For the Bible tells us:

1 Corinthians 2:16
For who hath known the mind of the Lord, that he may instruct Him? But we have the mind of Christ.

We did not receive the mind of Christ to be passive or indifferent. We received the mind of Christ to think like He does. And if you never thought of that, it may be that you have not been using the mind of Christ. It's okay. It's not too late. You can start right now. When you were born again, you did not become a mindless robot. Quite the opposite. Imagine, now you can think in ways you weren't even capable of before, even to discern and to judge rightly. That's another way that you can prove all things. Think! Think about what you are hearing. Some things you hear will not ring true. Don't ignore that or dismiss it from your mind. Take that as a signal to follow-up and in the light of the truth of God's word, examine carefully what you've heard. Refuse to be a passive listener. Engage your thinking capacity. You have the mind of Christ. Use it.

Patient Examination

I remember a long time ago I wasn't feeling well, so I went to a local clinic. (Thank God for past tense.) I was expecting a thorough examination, maybe some bloodwork or something, for them to check me out properly. By the time I went in and sat down, the doctor came and listened through his stethoscope to my breathing. Then he checked my throat, and that was it. The examination was over. Needless to say, I walked out the same way I walked in and with nothing to show for it.

That's how some people treat the Word of God. You can't just walk in and walk out when it comes to testing what you hear. You must make a patient, careful and thorough examination of those things you are testing to be true. That requires time and effort. The Apostle Paul instructed Timothy:

2 Timothy 2:15
Study to shew thyself approved unto God, a workman that needeth not to be ashamed, rightly dividing the word of truth.

The word for 'approved' right there is the same word *dókimos* from which we get the word *dokimazó* as in "prove" all things. Do you see the connection? Testing to approve is the requirement, and you need patience to carry out.

Accept and Reject

I want you to notice something here. The command in 1 Thessalonians 5:21 is in two parts. The first part is to "prove all things." Remember, you are required to prove, carefully examine, investigate, test anything presented to you as coming from God. Then you will be able to carry out the second part of the instruction, "hold fast to what is good."

The word translated 'good' is *kalós*, and it refers to good in the sense of being genuine and approved. When you hear preaching, teaching, or prophesying, pull out your spiritual sieve, put what you hear in there, shake it until only what lines up with the Word comes through, and hold fast to that. Eat the fish, leave the bones. Be a discriminating christians and don't hold onto everything you hear unless it is approved.

It is no secret that there are those who go around preaching, teaching, and prophesying that God said this or that when He hasn't said any such thing. That is why Paul had to tell us to test what we hear. As much as we would like it not to be the case, false preachers, teachers, and prophets do exist. That's why the Bible says:

1 John 4:1
Beloved, believe not every spirit, but try [*dokimazó*] the spirits whether they are of God: because many false prophets [*and teachers* emphasis added] are gone out into the world.

The same instruction that Apostle Paul gave in 1 Thessalonians 5:21 is repeated here. Examine everything in the light of God's Word that is purported to be coming to you from God. And after doing that, you are only required to hold onto what is approved as good. Otherwise, reject it.

The Guidance of the Spirit

No method of proving all things would be successful without the Holy Spirit. He is the Spirit of Truth and the One who guides us into all truth. Jesus said:

John 16:13
Howbeit when He, the Spirit of truth, is come, He will guide you into all truth...

When we don't prove all things, we insult the Spirit of Truth. We grieve Him by showing a reckless disregard for what He came to do and denying Him the privilege of leading us into truth. The Holy Spirit leads, but His leading is fruitless if we don't follow. The Holy Spirit is your teacher. He is the One who helps you understand the Word. But how can He teach without a willing student? He will be grieved. As your Guide, He has a wealth of experience and information to share with you, but He will be left unfulfilled if you do not come to Him and accept His guidance.

Remember that the Holy Spirit is the author and inspirer of the Scriptures. If ever there was a person to help you to verify and approve what lines up with the Word, it is Him. Give Him the joy of doing that. As you do, you will never be disadvantaged or deceived, because as He guides you into all truth, He will at the same time guide you away from all deception.

[1]Strong, James. *Strong's Exhaustive Concordance of the Bible*. Abingdon Press, 1890.

CHAPTER FIFTEEN

Abstain from All Appearance of Evil

There is an awareness of the presence of the Holy Spirit that is essential to maintain. We spoke of this in the chapter that deals with "pray without ceasing." Such an awareness requires faith because though you may not see Him with your physical eyes as I did that October day, He is more real and more present than anything you can see. The Bible tells us:

Hebrews 11:1
Now faith is the substance of things hoped for, the evidence of things not seen.

Through the spiritual substance of faith, you will be able to interact with the Holy Spirit, conversing with Him, listening to Him, laughing with Him, involving Him in your daily activities. As we move now towards the end of our discourse, I will show you how faith, along with self-control and goodness work together in carrying out the final instruction: abstain from all appearance of evil.

The Pain of Being Ignored

I want you to imagine this. Let's say you are married to the love of your life. And from the day you were married, you never talk to them; you never eat with them; you never say good morning or goodnight; you never ask how their day is going; you speak about them, but you never speak to them; you never acknowledge their presence; you never introduce them to anyone; you never tell them that you love them. You live every day as if that person doesn't even exist, yet every day you are using their resources to your benefit. What kind of relationship would you call that? Can you imagine ever treating the love of your life that way? Yet, that is how the Holy Spirit is treated by most Christians on a daily basis. The Holy Spirit is the most ignored Person of the Godhead, yet He is the One most present with us here on Earth. Without Him you would have never come to a saving knowledge of Jesus Christ and become a part of the family of God. Without Him you could never know or understand spiritual things. Without the Holy Spirit, you would never receive any spiritual gift or function in any measure of power; you could not love; you would not even exist.

The Holy Spirit loves you more than you could ever imagine. And He's right there with you now. Your relationship with Him is the most important relationship on Earth. Value it above all others. Think of it. The most important Person on Earth, the third Person of the Godhead, desires to be your best Friend. That is almost too good to be true!

Understanding the Mysterious

It is rare to find loyal people much less those who you can call true friends. When you do, you treasure them and the relationship you have. You do everything in your power to preserve and protect that relationship. It is from this vantage point that we will look at the final instruction:

1 Thessalonians 5:22
Abstain from all appearance of evil.

The word "appearance" in the King James Version isn't a mistranslation, but it does gravely cloud the meaning. In an attempt to explain what this verse means, many people say if something appears to be evil, then we must abstain from it.

However, this is an extremely subjective interpretation of the scripture because the person who is explaining the passage determines what appears to be evil and what doesn't.

The perspective of such people is usually based on what they don't like. If they don't like the colour red, they say wearing red is an "appearance of evil." If they don't like to see people driving luxury cars, when they see a preacher driving a Lamborghini, they say that's an "appearance of evil." Anything they disapprove of that engages others is deemed to be an appearance of evil. Do you see how this way of thinking would make it impossible for us to carry out the instruction to abstain from all appearance of evil? It is impossible to abstain from everything that looks like evil when understood in this way.

The problem with the way most Christians interpret this verse is they automatically think about a bunch of rules, do's and don'ts relating to keeping away from what is considered or is evil. Most people focus on the "evil" part, but it is really not about that. To understand the thrust of what this verse is about and personalize it, I want you to keep one question in mind as you read it: *Why*? There's a 'why' behind every 'what,' and if you understand the 'why,' it will make the 'what' that much more easily understood. We must first understand that the context of the verse is relating to verse 19 which says:

1 Thessalonians 5:19
Quench not the Spirit.

All that we have discussed in this book so far from verses 12 up through our current verse 22 is in light of this instruction to not quench the Spirit. To fully understand why this is important, you need to know something about His nature which is where most Christians have a problem. To most Christians, the Holy Spirit is mysterious. If this is not the case with you, before you are too hard on the others, let me explain why others may think this way.

In the Bible, we see God speaking about Himself. He reveals His names; He speaks of His character; He declares His power. Even with Jesus, we see Him talking about Himself, who He is and what He came to do. But when it comes to the Holy Spirit, Jesus said of Him:

John 16:13
He will not speak of Himself.

The Holy Spirit does not talk about Himself in scripture. That is what makes symbolism that relates to Him so essential. Many symbols have been used to represent Him: wind, fire, water, rain, rivers, oil, wine, a seal. But of all of His symbolic representations, the one I would like to expound on the most is the dove.

It's of paramount importance to note before I go any further that the Holy Spirit IS NOT A DOVE. There are Christians who actually think if they see a white dove they've seen the Holy Spirit. Some people have gone further to put doves on logos saying it's a picture of the Holy Spirit when it definitely is not. The dove is symbolic.

Let me show you this scripture as an analogy just to make this clearer;

Jeremiah 50:17
Israel *is* a scattered sheep; the lions have driven *him* away...

In this verse the Israelites are being symbolically referred to as sheep. If you were asked today to point to a Jewish person would you point to sheep? Of course you wouldn't! Do you get the sense? So let's delve a little deeper on the use of the dove as a symbol of the Holy Spirit with the understanding that He is not a dove.

Every other symbol used to represent the Holy Spirit is inanimate except the dove. Of all of the living things that He could have chosen to represent Him, why the dove? Most people identify the symbolism of the dove with the inauguration of Jesus' public ministry. So, let's start there by looking at Matthew's account of what happened:

Matthew 3:13-16
13 Then cometh Jesus from Galilee to Jordan unto John, to be baptized of him. 14 But John forbad Him, saying, I have need to be baptized of Thee, and comest Thou to me? 15 And Jesus answering said unto him, 'Suffer it to be so now: for thus it becometh us to fulfil all righteousness.' Then he suffered Him. 16 And Jesus, when He was baptized, went up straightway out of the water: and, lo, the heavens were opened unto Him, and *He saw the Spirit of God descending like a dove, and lighting upon Him* [emphasis added].

Now, before we go any further, we need to clear up a misconception concerning this representation as a dove. Let me explain what I mean in the simplest of terms. If I say the apple is like an orange, you understand that I do not mean an apple is an orange. To say that something is like something else means that there is some characteristic they share in common. In the example I gave you, an apple and orange are like each other in that both are fruit. But the understanding is they are not the same but alike in some way. Therefore, when the verse says that the Holy Spirit descended like or in the form of a dove, it is with the understanding that the Holy Spirit is not a dove, but there is something dove-like about His nature and descent. Are you with me so far?

Like A Dove

Everything the Holy Spirit does is intentional and significant. The Holy Spirit could have chosen to descend in any form whatsoever. He could have even created a form that never existed before. But He chose to descend like a dove. That lets us know that there is something noteworthy about this particular symbol, the dove. Let's look at a few characteristics of the dove, and in so doing, we will learn something about the nature of the Holy Spirit.

One notable thing about the dove is that it is clean by nature. In the romantic biblical book of Song of Solomon, a dove is used to represent an undefiled lover:

Song of Solomon 6:9
My dove, my undefiled is but one...

In the Old Testament, the dove is one of the clean birds used for sacrifices. And when the dove was released from the ark after the flood, it would not land where there was filth. We see this in the book of Genesis where the dove was first mentioned. Let's take a look:

Genesis 8:6-9
6 And it came to pass at the end of forty days, that Noah opened the window of the ark which he had made: 7 And he sent forth a raven, which went forth to and fro, until the waters were dried up from off the earth. 8 Also he sent forth a dove from him, to see if the waters were abated from off the face of the ground; 9 But the dove found no rest for the sole of her foot, and she returned unto him into the ark, for the waters were on the face of the whole earth: then he put forth his hand, and took her, and pulled her in unto him into the ark.

Notice there that the raven, a "dirty" bird which eats carrion, did not return to the ark. It was comfortable amongst the filth and dead things left in the wake of the flood. The dove, however, being a clean bird, could not find any place to rest under those conditions. So, when we see the Holy Spirit represented as a dove, we are mindful that He is pure, undefiled, and perfect. He is holy, completely separate from the filth of sin. Apostle Paul says:

2 Corinthians 7:1 AMPC
Therefore, since these [great] promises are ours, beloved, let us cleanse ourselves from everything that contaminates and defiles body and spirit, and bring [our] consecration to completeness in the [reverential] fear of God.

The Holy Spirit is with us. The question remains, is He able to rest with us? He has made us His dwelling place, but He cannot rest where filthiness and dead things are. Therefore, for us to maintain fellowship with Him, He desires us to "cleanse ourselves from everything that contaminates and defiles body and spirit."

Another essential characteristic of a dove is that it is peaceful and gentle by nature. Jesus is the first person mentioned in the Bible on whom the Holy Spirit descended and remained. In times before, the Holy Spirit would come upon people, but He never remained. He would come, empower them for some assignment, and then leave. But on Jesus, He remained. Notice that when Jesus sent out His disciples, He told them to be "harmless as doves." Watch what the Bible says:

Matthew 10:16
Behold, I send you forth as sheep in the midst of wolves: be ye therefore wise as serpents, and harmless as doves.

I want to point out something very interesting here about the word 'harmless.' When we see that word, we may automatically think it means unable or unwilling to do harm. But the Greek gives us greater insight. In the Greek, 'harmless' is the word *akéraios* and it means 'pure' like refined metal that is free of impurities. It also means 'unmixed' like the best wine that is undiluted. In summary, harmless means without a mixture of evil or innocent. That is what the Holy Spirit is like.

All Appearance of Evil

Having seen something of the characteristics of the Holy Spirit as symbolized by a dove, now we are ready to look again at our focus verse:

1 Thessalonians 5:22
Abstain from all appearance of evil.

Evil has an appearance. It is not ethereal or amorphous. It takes form, and that form can be seen. But I do not mean in the way you might be thinking. What we are addressing here is not evil itself, because as Christians who are born of the Spirit, we innately and instinctively know that we ought not to fellowship with evil. The Bible says:

2 Corinthians 6:14
What communion [fellowship] hath light with darkness?

Your *koinonia* or fellowship is to be with the Holy Spirit, not with the works of darkness. That is not the evil to which Paul is referring per se. He is not referring to an action, a work of evil. He is referring to that which is evil because of its effect or influence. To explain what I mean, let us look at one more characteristic of the dove.

Hosting the Holy Spirit

I love nature. I enjoy spending time in the wild. I can enjoy a parade of different species of birds. I watch them, and sometimes they watch me too. Every now and again, a dove will stop by for a visit. While I am quiet and undisturbed, they are content to remain where they are. But if I make a startling movement, they will quickly retreat. The dove is that way. It likes peace. The dove is, in fact, the global symbol for peace.

Here's the key: if you want to host the Holy Spirit properly, your fellowship with Him must be at peace, undisturbed. That requires temperance (self-control). In his critical commentary on the Greek New Testament, concerning 1 Thessalonians 5:22 Henry Alford wrote:

> It is not against being deceived by false appearance, nor against giving occasion by behaviour which appears like evil, that he is cautioning them, but merely to distinguish and hold fast that which is good, and to reject that which is evil.[1]

You see, there is an effort that is required on your part to reject evil and maintain your undisturbed fellowship with the Holy Spirit. You must allow self-control, *enkráteia*, the hand of your spirit to pull you away from anything that breaks the bond of peace. Apostle Paul says it this way:

Ephesians 4:3
Endeavouring to keep the unity of the Spirit in the bond of peace.

Like enjoying the dove outside my window, peace is the bond that maintains the fellowship with the Holy Spirit. Paul says do everything you can, make every effort to maintain the unity of the Spirit. Don't break your bond of peace with Him. In light of

Hello Holy Spirit

everything we have talked about in this book that keeps us from grieving the Holy Spirit and disturbing that peace between us, make every effort to do those things.

The evil that we must abstain is anything that takes the form of that which causes the peaceful union between you and the Holy Spirit to be disturbed. The word 'abstain' is *apechó* in the Greek which is derived from two words: *apo* and *echo*. We have seen and discussed *echo* in a few of the previous chapters. In short, it means 'to hold.' But this word *apo* is where the secret lies. In its most literal sense, it means 'away from,' hence the general meaning of 'abstain' when *apo* is combined with *echo* is to 'hold away from.' But *apo* is used more specifically to denote any kind of separation of one thing from another by which the union or fellowship of the two is destroyed. Therefore, the evil to be abstained is anything that interferes with, separates, or threatens to destroy your fellowship with the Holy Spirit. If you find a verse in scripture that lets you know that something grieves or quenches the Holy Spirit, stay away from that thing it talks about. Exercise self-control whenever necessary, and don't allow anything to disturb the peace of your relationship with Him.

Open the Door

I will never forget one particular morning when I was spending time with the Holy Spirit. I was looking out of the window, and it was as if I could feel what He was feeling. It's hard for me to talk about it, and even writing about it reminds me of what I felt that day. It was deep sadness. I asked Him what the matter was, and this is what He said.

"I have taken Jesus to the door of the hearts of many, and they have let Him in, and I'm very glad about that."

He continued,

"But many times as they open the door of their hearts to Him, they leave Me standing there."

I wept because I felt, at least to some small degree, His pain. It was in that moment that I began to understand how deeply the Holy Spirit longs to fellowship and have an intimate friendship with us. As I said in an earlier chapter, love is manifested and demonstrated in goodness, agathósuné, which is also translated 'generosity.' When you walk in the Spirit, you walk in love which manifests itself in generosity. Be generous to the Holy Spirit. Invest in and safeguard your relationship with Him. This is the ultimate form of goodness.

What Shall We Say About These Things

Remember everything we have been going through in these passages and what the Holy Spirit taught me on that day simply magnified what he had written through Paul to the Galatians. Instructing them how to walk in the spirit, and in the book of Thessalonians he went into details pointing out the things in the church that were hindering and quenching the Spirit of God. It all boils down to walking in love having the fruit of the spirit in your life. The love of God is shed abroad in our hearts by His Spirit, and when you choose to yield to Him all these things become second nature. Not only do you live in the spirit but you will walk in the spirit and nothing shall be impossible for you.

Galatians 5:22-23
But the fruit of the Spirit is love, joy, peace, longsuffering, gentleness, goodness, faith, meekness, temperance: against such there is no law.

This book is about the Holy Spirit and how you can make Him your best Friend. He is the Friend who sticks closer than a brother (Proverbs 18:24). I have shown you, as He showed me, ways that will avoid grieving Him and causing Him to withdraw. These are the things that would harm your relationship with Him. If you do not know Him as a friend, I plead with you, don't leave Him waiting outside the door of your heart any longer. He's been eagerly waiting for this moment. Knowing Him and walking with Him is the key to a successful life. Right now where you are, by faith, know that He is there. Smile at Him and say, "Hello, Holy Spirit."

Lightning Source UK Ltd.
Milton Keynes UK
UKHW012016041119
352887UK00002B/2/P